Rudolf and Ippai Attena

SAITO Hiroshi

Translated by Deborah Iwabuchi and Kazuko Enda
Illustrated by Hanmo Sugiura

Kodansha

挿画・杉浦 範茂

Contents

Prologue 5

Chapter 1 An Unexpected Trip 7

Chapter 2 A Big Town 10

Chapter 3 Ippai Attena 14

Chapter 4 The Witch's House 20

Chapter 5 Where Did I Come From? 26

Chapter 6 Cream Stew and Education 31

Chapter 7 The Fish Shop and Ippai Attena 35

Chapter 8 Education 39

Chapter 9 Milk and the Blurry Moon 43

Chapter 10 What Butchy Had to Say 47

Chapter 11 Ippai Attena Gets Angry 56

Chapter 12 Ippai Attena's Secret 61

Chapter 13 School Books and Education 68

Chapter 14 Youth Is Wasted on the Young 73

Chapter 15 Boss and Mr. Bear 78

Chapter 16 The Library and Human Progress 84

Chapter 17 The Bear's Den 88

Chapter 18 Big Discovery 92

Chapter 19 Expectation, Disappointment, and then Hope ... 97

Chapter 20 What the Typhoon Brought 103

Chapter 21 Ippai Attena's Hard-luck Story 115

Chapter 22 Good News 119

Chapter 23 Preparing for Departure 123

Chapter 24 Foul Play 128

Chapter 25 The Morning of My Departure 141

Chapter 26 Two Avengers and *Chushingura* 145

Author's Afterword 154

Notes 156

Prologue

I'm Rudolf and I wrote this book. I live right here in Japan. If you've ever heard any Japanese names before, you might think Rudolf doesn't sound Japanese. Well, you're right. Neither my name nor I am Japanese. But I'm *not* not Japanese either.

Are you confused? You shouldn't be. The only reason this doesn't make sense is because you think only humans can write. And that's where you're wrong.

Are you wondering if I'm an alien from outer space? No, I'm nothing like that. I don't know if there is such a thing as aliens, but what I do know is that you'd be shocked speechless if you were just walking around town and happened to see a space creature in the shadows of a postbox, or looked up to find one on a roof. And so would I. I'd probably faint if I saw an alien with a huge head wearing some kind of silvery space suit and floating in mid-air.

Don't get me wrong, I'm not against a good eye-opener every once in a while, but I won't be having that effect on you. Still, I might surprise you late at night when you're walking down a dark street. Down close to the ground, you might see two shiny spots. Those are the eyes of creatures like me. But we're not trying to shock anyone. Our eyes just reflect light and shine blue.

Got it yet? I'm a cat.

So maybe now you're wondering how a cat can write a book. You're probably thinking it's impossible. Humans can be so cynical. Always doubting new things they hear. Hundreds of years ago, there was this guy, Copernicus. He said the earth orbited the sun, and not the other way around. Nobody believed him—at first. Lots of people laughed and some even got hopping mad.

But you know, humans don't know how to read or write until they learn. It's the same with cats, but harder. I mean, it's hard for humans too. I've seen some of the scores kids get on tests, so I know it's not easy for you. Just think what it must be like for a cat. I'll tell you what. If you read this whole book, you'll find out how I learned to read and write like a human. I don't expect you to understand it all right away. All I need you to know is that my name is Rudolf and I'm a cat. And I can write. And one other thing. I'm a black cat. A black cat named Rudolf.

Chapter 1

An Unexpected Trip

Whoosh! A stone the size of a golf ball flew past my head. Rats! He'd found me. I should have taken the stolen fish to a quieter spot. But I was starving. I never should have tried to scarf it down so fast. There was no time now, I realized, and picked up my half-eaten smelt and ran.

"Thief! Thief! That cat did it again!"

I could hear the voice coming closer.

Bonk! The second rock missed again. Worse aim than the first one. At least he wasn't going for my legs. Those were the worst. If one ever got me in the head, well of course it could knock me right out. But that never happened. The first one would fly over my head. The second time, they'd try to aim better, but they wouldn't put as much power into it. If the first one hit my legs, I could still limp away, but I'd be an easier target and then the next rock could be lethal.

Whatever. When rocks started flying, you had to hightail it. And you had to dodge to the left or the right of the direction they were heading in. There was no stopping for a breath or to think about strategy. A moving target was harder to hit. But you know that, right?

Run. Run. To the left. To the right.

I headed for human crowds. That was a good way to stop the rocks. Evening shoppers, always a good bet. All you had to do was slip in and you'd be home free. I sped out from behind the fish shop and into the crowded street.

I zipped through legs, most of them as thick as big daikon radishes, and just kept running. Whoops, a pointy heel. One of those steps on you and, wow, it hurts.

It wasn't the first time that fishmonger had launched rocks at me, but he usually quit after one or two. Today he wasn't giving up. Wasn't he busy enough without chasing a cat? Must have hit a nerve today.

If I could just turn the corner at the flower shop, there was an alley with a fence at the end of it, and beyond the fence lots of places to hide. I mean it wasn't my house or my garden, but you know us cats, your yard is my yard. The whole town is our yard. But that's enough small talk for now, it was time to make a dash.

I took a wide right and almost ran into a bucket from the flower shop. There were only a couple more meters to the fence. And—no! The little fence had been replaced with a concrete wall. If I backed up a bit and took a run at it, I should have been able to jump over it, but there was no time. The alley I'd just turned into was a dead end. Should I go for the wall, or make a U-turn? Just then, I heard a crash and a splash.

"Ouch!"

I whipped around to see the fishmonger on the ground covered in water. He'd tripped over that bucket.

This was my chance. I reversed direction and headed straight toward my pursuer who was laid flat out on the ground. He tried to jump up, but I flew right over his head and back out into the shopping street.

Finally, safe! I thought, but I was sadly mistaken. The fishmonger pulled himself to his feet with a furious expression on his face. He picked up a mop and took off after me, the water squishing in his boots. This looked bad. I had to get away.

Then I saw it. Just beyond the fish shop, there was a truck with a cover on the back. The driver was just getting in to leave. I could see an opening in the cover—I ran for it. Behind me I could hear the mop whooshing through the air, water splashing in the boots, and the fishmonger yelling unintelligibly.

It was three meters to the truck. The engine revved up. Two meters. The truck pulled away from the curb. Jump!

Just as I leaped into the air, something whapped the back of my head and I fell into the back of the truck. Everything went black. I wasn't sure if the drone I could hear was from the engine of the truck or the inside of my head.

Chapter 2

A Big Town

I could still hear that drone. It seemed far off, and then the noise got closer and closer until it was right inside my ear. That was when I woke up. I was hearing the sound of the truck I found myself in.

My head was heavy and my mind was foggy. I stretched out my right front leg. Then my left one. Then my back legs—both at once. All of them seemed to be working fine, so I figured I could stand up. Willing myself up and pressing on my back legs, I wobbled a little, but I was finally up on my feet just fine.

Now what exactly had happened? I tried to remember. Oh yeah. The instant I jumped toward the back of the truck, the fishmonger got me with his mop. Right in the head. And that was it . . . until now.

It was dim inside the truck, but I could see a little light in the back. It must be coming through the space I had managed to leap through. The floor of the truck was shaking, but I made my unsteady way toward the light. I put my face up to it, and could feel the flapping of the truck cover over my head and the wind in my face. We must be going pretty fast.

I shoved my head out a little further and was blinded by sunlight. It was morning. That meant I'd been knocked out all night. Had the truck been traveling the whole time? Where was I?

The scenery racing by was completely unfamiliar. And this road was so wide. Something else bothered me, but I couldn't quite put my finger on it.

Then I figured it out. No people. Or bicycles either. Nothing but cars. And all going so fast. I also noticed the truck didn't make any stops—no traffic signals either. It was weird. I'd never seen anything like it.

Then the truck began to slow down, pulled under a big gate and stopped. I peeked out from under the cover and saw the driver paying money to some man in a uniform. Must be buying something. But the uniformed guy didn't give the driver anything. Just a little piece of paper. The truck started running again.

Rats! I should've jumped out while it was stopped, I thought. Now it was too dangerous to try. But wait! I'd been in this truck for hours. What would I gain from getting right off? Here I was in a new place. Maybe I should look around a little first. I leaned out from under the cover a little further and tried to get a good look.

The road seemed to be very high, and there was this huge town underneath it. A lot bigger than where I was from. I loved to look down from high places. There was a mountain just outside of my town; you could climb up it or take a ropeway from the foot of the mountain. It was just about fifteen minutes from my house—er—my human's house. There was a park and I went there all the time. The guy who ran the fish shop really hated me, but I was friends with the girl at the ropeway station. Well, actually she lived next door to me and waved to me every morning. I'd be sitting outside and she'd say, "See you later, Rudolf!" She'd even rub my head before she headed off.

I wondered where she went every day, so one day I followed her. That's how I found out she worked for the ropeway. I noticed the park, and after that, I'd go visit there sometimes.

Once, I was at the pond in the park trying to catch a goldfish, when I heard a voice.

"Hey, look! It's Rudolf!" I turned around and there was my neighbor. I hadn't even noticed. I was so busy trying to catch that fish. I thought I was in big trouble, but she picked me up.

"I've got something lots better than catching goldfish!" she said, and carried me to the ropeway. "No customers today, so let's take a ride!" She carried me on board with one hand and closed the door with the other. The car swayed a little and slowly began to move—straight up, all the way to the mountain peak.

After that, I was hooked. I went back lots of times to ride with her. Since the ropeway ran on a schedule, there was always a little time for me to look around at the top before going back down. The girl took a break while I walked around. There was an old castle and I could look down from it at the whole town.

That's how I knew how big the town was. The one I was looking at now from inside the truck was too huge to even compare. It just went on and on and on, no matter how far the truck went. From my mountain I could see fields where the houses stopped, but not here. Just houses and more houses and other buildings. Where was I?

Eventually, the truck went off at an angle and then down a hill, and finally we were back on streets where there were people and bicycles. The truck stopped, and then ran a while, stopped again a few times, and then turned right, and left, and finally pulled into a big parking lot.

When the engine turned off, I figured it was time for me to get moving.

Chapter 3

Ippai Attena

The driver got out and went into a nearby building, so I decided this was my chance. Just as I was about to jump through the opening in the cover, I stepped on something. It was the smelt I'd stolen from the fish shop the day before. I realized I was starving. But if I stopped to eat the fish, the driver might come back and then what? I didn't want to leave it either. I'd just have to take it along with me and find a quiet spot to scarf it down.

I grabbed the fish, stuck my head out from under the cover, looked around to make sure the coast was clear, and jumped out. I ran past several other trucks and toward the wall surrounding the parking lot. I found a hole, and squeezed through into an alley. Should I go right or left? The right would take me back to the main road. I'd already been there, so I took a left.

Then I heard a voice.

"Hey, kid! Little stroll after your drive?"

I looked up to see a huge striped cat. Jumping down to land right next to me, he growled again.

"Think you can walk around here for free?"

I could see I was in a fight-or-flight situation. I

wondered if the cat was from the neighborhood. If I tried to escape, he'd know where to cut me off. I could try and fight him, but he was easily twice my size. Neither option seemed promising. I stood there thinking, the whole time staring at the big cat's face.

Maybe he got tired of waiting. He came closer and stuck his face in mine. "Huh, I knew there was something strange. Not from around here, eh? Otherwise, you would've run when you saw me." I still didn't have anything to say, so he went on. "You've got smelt there, boy. Leave it behind and take off. I'm tired of looking at you."

I'd gone to a lot of trouble to get this fish this far. Now if he'd said he was hungry and asked me to split it with him, maybe I would've. On the other hand, I hated to lose the fish. I'd come all this way in a truck, had no idea what was going on, and now this gigantic cat was shaking me down. What was going to happen next? Trying a new tack, I put the fish down and stuck my nose in the air.

"You want it so bad, you can have it! Not like you're asking anyway."

To tell the truth, I was about to cry. It wasn't just losing the meal; it was all so humiliating. Cats don't have laws like humans. It's every beast for himself. And it's all about power. Or you can use your head to keep from getting caught in the first place and avoid any kind of fight.

But I'd already failed at that. When I got out of the truck, I'd been checking for humans and hadn't even noticed this big lug. It was the same when I'd got caught stealing the fish—a total lack of attention. Why was it always so tough for us little guys?

"Never expected to find country bandits in such a big town, but I guess there'll always be bullies who like to pick on someone smaller," I mumbled to myself, just as I realized the cat had probably heard. It was bound to make him even angrier. Sticking around was not a wise idea—I'd have to take off. I took a few steps before I heard a voice behind me.

"Not so fast."

I kept going.

"I said, not so fast!"

I told myself not to look back. The instant I turned, he'd jump and he'd have his claws in my face. I needed to get as much distance as possible before the attack. Judging from his size, he couldn't leap further than about two meters without a running start. I needed to get at least that far ahead. Then I'd turn to look.

When cats jump, we can change direction once in mid-air. I knew that if I leaped to the left, my opponent would twist that way too, so I planned to feint left and dash to the right. When he tried to do the same, he'd land off balance and fall on his enormous gut, and hopefully, sprain a leg or two. That was when I'd make my escape.

"Hey wait! I said wait!" From the sound of his voice, I guessed I was two meters ahead of him. Now! I turned to look as I feinted left. Instead of leaping, though, the cat just stood there looking at me.

"What d'you think you're doing? Seriously. You thought I was going to jump over there, so you were gonna dodge and run in the other direction? Like I'd ever fall for that old trick."

My strategy had failed miserably, but I didn't want to admit it.

"Got nothin' better to do than stand there?" I snarled.

"On your way somewhere?" The striped cat wasn't budging.

"None of your business. You got my food, what else do you want?"

"You oughta be more afraid of me, you brat."

"Why d'you think you got the fish, eh? Now what d'you want?"

The big cat left my smelt behind and walked slowly over to me. This was never good. The closer a cat got, the easier it was to move in for the kill. I was ready for the worst. He was within reach of me now. I cringed and closed my eyes tight.

"Relax, punk," said the cat. "Just so you know, most cats take off as soon as they know I'm around. None of them try to talk tough like you. I'll give you credit for that. I've never lost—even to a dog—and everyone around here knows it. But slapping around a shrimp like you would make me look bad. I'll even give you back your smelt."

Now it was my turn to be surprised. What was the deal with this bully? If he was just going to give back the fish, why'd he take it in the first place? But as long as he wasn't on the attack, I wasn't going to back down.

"It's yours, ya big lunk. You took it once and now I'm giving it to you."

"Hold your horses, odd job. What is it with you anyway? I take it and you complain, I give it back and now you don't want it."

"Who's the odd job? You make me give it to you, and now you don't want it." I tried to say "odd job" the same way he did and I nailed it. I had to laugh. The big cat laughed too.

"Ha ha ha, you're as odd as they come. What's your name?" he asked.

"Rudolf. What about you?"

"Me, er, well, *ippai attena*," he mumbled.

"What kinda name is Ippai Attena?" I asked.

"Don't be stupid. There's no such name. But if you like it, you can call me that. Now take your fish. Here."

"Now who's stupid, Mr. Ippai Attena? I told you once that I don't take things back I've given away. If you don't want my fish, leave it there."

Ippai Attena thought about it a moment or two and finally spoke.

"In that case, I'll take it. But don't go telling people I shook down a squirt like you for a smelt. I've got my reputation to think of. I was just trying to scare you off. You shoulda taken your itsy bitsy little fish and run off to start with."

"Shoulda thought of that before," I retorted. "But I won't be mouthing off to your cronies. Never met them anyway. I'm outta here."

"Not so fast," said Ippai Attena. "Let's take a little walk." And off he trotted with my fish in his mouth. I thought a second. I was new in town and had to admit I didn't have anything better to do—and this Ippai Attena was turning out to be an interesting character. When I didn't move, he stopped and turned around.

"A walk!" he growled, and I followed.

Chapter 4

The Witch's House

Walking behind Ippai Attena with his tail in my face, I realized just how big he was. I was still a kid, but I knew that when cats become adults, their faces start to balloon. If all you see is their faces, some cats look enormous, but up close they're not so impressive. This Ippai Attena had a big face, but the rest of his body was massive too. His fur was grayish brown with black stripes. I'd heard there were animals somehow related to cats called tigers, but I'd never seen one. Striped cats like Ippai Attena were called tiger cats because they looked like those other animals. Real tigers were bigger than big dogs, I'd heard. Ippai Attena wasn't huge like that . . . but it got me wondering. What kind of an animal was a tiger if it was bigger than my companion here *and* bigger than a dog?

I thought about it as I walked, and when Ippai Attena stopped and whipped around to look at me, I almost thought he was a real tiger, and I yowled in alarm. He put down the smelt.

"Now what's the matter, half pint?" he asked.

"Whaddaya mean? Why'd you just stop and turn around like that?"

"We might be a little early," he said.

"Early? Early for what?"

"Food, dimwit."

"I was wondering where you were walking off to like some big shot. So this is it, you're gonna treat me to a meal?"

"We're not heading to the beach for sun and fun, knucklehead. Of course it's food!"

The truth was, I was starving. I'd take a fishtail or squid head, I didn't care. I just wanted to eat, and the sooner the better. Of course, I didn't want to look too anxious in front of Ippai Attena.

"I don't need you to feed me, bait breath," I said. "I can find food on my own."

"Doesn't work like that," he replied. "Once I've decided to treat someone, I do it no matter what. But I'm telling you it's too early for lunch. Let's make another stop first." Without checking with me, Ippai Attena picked up the smelt and headed off again.

We slipped under some fences, zipped through an alley or two and finally arrived in front of an old broken-down one-story house. Sandwiched between concrete buildings, it didn't get much sunlight. Some of the windows were broken and patched up with duct tape. The wooden front door looked like it would cave in with a half-hearted kick. Did anyone live here? From where we were, I could see a light on inside even though it was the middle of the day. Someone might be in there, although the tattered curtains made it impossible to get a good look. What were we doing here?

My companion went right up to the door, stuck out a paw and began to scratch it.

Scritch, scritch, scratch, scratch. The motion made the window in the door rattle. *Scritch, rattle, rattle, scratch, rattle, rattle.* Nobody answered.

Scratch, rattle, scritch, rattle. Was he planning to work up an appetite at this haunted house? Or did he live here?

When no one answered, Ippai Attena began to screech. *Mee-YOW! Meeeee-YOOW!* And the whole time he kept scratching on the door. The sound of his claws, the window shaking and the yowling made a real ruckus. *Scritch, rattle, rattle, Mee-YOW! Scratch, scratch, rattle, Meeeee-YOOW!* On and on.

Then, all of a sudden, the door opened. So sudden, I thought Ippai Attena would fly straight through it. Who should appear at the door of that dark, dingy house, but a wrinkled old hunched-over hag. She had a cloth wrapped around her head—she had to be a witch!

"Who's making all that racket?" she called out in a shaky voice, and looked sharply around. In her hands was . . . a broom! I knew it, a bonafide witch! She was going to take off on that broom at any second. Ippai Attena must be her cat. She'd probably make me do her bidding too. Or, or she might boil and eat me! Here I was, sure I was going to get a good meal but, no, I was the one on the menu! Maybe she'd simmer me with potatoes in a curry. I hated potatoes, and I didn't want to be cooked up with any. Between the terror and my empty stomach, my legs gave out from under me.

"Oh, Tiger, it's you," the witch said, in a friendly tone. "It's been a while, hasn't it?" Then she bent down and patted Ippai Attena on the head.

What did she call him? Tiger? So that's what he really was. That explained the size—he wasn't a cat after all. Maybe she'd put a spell on him to look like a cat so he wouldn't get in trouble. She'd probably recite some kind of magic words and turn him back into a real tiger—make him even bigger than he was now! Mee-*YOW*, mee-*YOW*, he'd howled. In a minute it was going to be *ROAR!* And then—then he'd come after me for sure!

"Tiger, did you bring me a little present? Now, wasn't that sweet of you. You're such a good boy. Thank you very much, and I appreciate it." She carefully picked up the smelt at Ippai Attena's feet. Probably going to use it in the broth for the curry, I thought.

As the witch petted the big cat, he mewed like a lovesick kitten. I just sat there waiting for him to start roaring and for his paws to grow as big as tree trunks. The witch finally noticed me there with him.

"Tiger, did you bring a little friend today? Oh dear me."

Oh dear me? What was she upset about? I was the one in trouble. I tried to say something—anything to save myself, but I was too scared to make a sound.

"Oh dear me," she repeated. "I don't have a thing in the house and it's too early for lunch."

I knew it! I was going to be lunch for Tiger and his witch. Potatoes and carrots—and me! All boiled up in a curry.

"Let me see what I can find," said the witch. "You two wait here."

She went back into the dingy house and the door banged shut behind her. This would be a good time to leave, I knew, but the instant I tried to make my move, Ippai Attena stepped on my tail with his paw.

"Where ya going, short stuff?" His gruff attitude was back; I was sure it must be time for him to turn into a tiger. And then the door creaked open again.

"It's all I've got." The witch was back. I didn't know what she had, because my eyes were squeezed shut. Probably a saw or an ax instead of that broom. She'd go straight for my neck with it. Then it would be the curry pot.

"Come on, eat!" It was Ippai Attena.

"I don't have all day, boys! Eat it up!" It was the witch. I felt the paw come off my tail, but since I was still straining to escape, I shot forward and ended up with my face against the doorstep. When I finally got a look at what was happening, the witch had something in her hand and she was feeding it to Ippai Attena. Not only that, but he was still a cat, not a tiger at all. The witch glanced over at me, and held out her other hand.

"This is for you. You're the first friend Tiger has ever brought with him. Your fur looks so clean. You can't be a stray. Eat up and go straight home, you hear?"

I peeked into the witch's hand. A dried sardine! It smelled like heaven. Wait, it wasn't one . . . there were two, wait . . . three, four . . . five in all! Ippai Attena had his head in the witch's hand and was happily munching away. I took a lick, and my terror dissolved as my appetite kicked in. I opened wide and took a big bite.

It was good. So good. I polished the sardines off, but Ippai Attena was faster. I was still eating, and he was already sitting there licking his chops. The witch stood up, shook her hands clean, and clapped.

"All right, then. Off with you! I've got lots to do. I can't stand here chatting all day. I was right in the middle of my housework." She went back into the house, closing the door with a bang.

Ippai Attena stood up, and said, "Now for the next place!"

I stood up and followed.

Chapter 5

Where Did I Come From?

"Hey, Mr. Ippai Attena, that was a great meal, but it was also the scariest thing that's ever happened to me. And now I know you're a witch's cat."

"Witch's cat? Who're you talking about? Not me, that's for sure. I don't belong to a witch—or anybody."

I could see that I was in real danger of getting on his nerves, but I still needed to ask a few questions.

"But she is a witch, right?"

"An old lady who gets on a broom to fly around in the sky? There's no such thing, you numbskull."

"I never believed in witches till I saw that old lady. She's gotta be one," I insisted. Ippai Attena just stared at me for a few seconds and then burst out laughing.

"HA HA ha ha ha ha, oh help, ha ha ha, *hoo, hooo,* ha, *haaaa.* Witch? Her? HEE HEE ha ha ha ho, ho, *oh, oh,* ah har har har!" Once he started, he didn't seem to be able to stop. He finally gave up even trying to stand and rolled over on his back right there on the side of the road. "Oh my, oh my, I haven't laughed like that in a long, long time. Hoo, ha, ha, ha. But I can see—ha ha ha—how she might look like a witch. And witches do have cats and bats and snakes. Hee, hee . . . that's too rich . . . ah, ha.

"But listen here, uh, what's your name again? Noodle? Poodle? Uh, it's on the tip of my tongue . . ."

"Rudolf!"

"All right, fine, Rudolf. I'll just call you Rudy. I can remember that. Anyway, here in Tokyo there are no witches. Maybe they still have them where you come from. Where'd you say you were from again?"

Now I was confused. The old lady was *not* a witch. And Ippai Attena was telling me this was a place called Tokyo. What and where was that? For the moment, I was speechless, so Ippai Attena started explaining.

"OK, let's say they have witches where you come from. But that lady we just saw isn't one. And I'm no witch's cat. Here in Tokyo, there're a lot of old people living alone like that. I go visit and she's always nice. She used to have rats—awful filthy things—and who got rid of 'em for her? Me! That's who! Now she's good for a bite or two whenever I stop by. But look, where are you from? It's got to be way out in the country if you've got witches. What's the name of the place?"

"It's called Third Street. But I've never seen a witch there."

"Third Street? We've got a Third Street right over there across the tracks. I've never seen the likes of you there. So which Third Street is it?"

I didn't know what Ippai Attena was talking about. I

knew I lived on Third Street; that was a fact. But it wasn't here, that much was sure.

"OK," said Ippai Attena, determined to get information I didn't have, "you're from Third Street. But Third Street where? Every city and town all over the country's got one or two or lots of them. Why are you here? You came in a truck, so you must have come a long way."

I still didn't know what he was talking about, but I figured it was time to tell him my whole story. How the fishmonger chased me and I ended up in the truck and woke up to find myself in the present location.

Ippai Attena listened to me talk, from start to finish. Then he looked at me, almost like he felt sorry for me, and sighed.

"So Rudolf, are you planning to go home?"

"Whaddaya think?" I didn't know whether to get mad or break down and cry. "Of course I am!"

"Aha. Look, I hate to be the one to tell you this, but it sounds awfully far away, and well, you don't even know the name of the place. Ya got to pin it down to a city and prefecture—then you can look for your Third Street."

Ippai Attena and I started walking and he explained the situation to me. It turned out that we were in a country called Japan and Japan was made up of prefectures and cities and all kinds of other places. Right now, we were in a big city called Tokyo. The part of

Tokyo we were in was Edogawa Ward, right on the eastern edge of it. Ippai Attena said the place I came from had to have a name too. Something-something City in Something-something Prefecture. Or something like that. And then there'd be another smaller something-something division that had my Third Street in it. The problem was, I didn't know the names of any of those something-somethings.

"And that's why you can't go home even if you want to," Ippai Attena concluded. "You're too far away—you drove all night in that truck."

Ippai Attena finally stopped talking and we were both quiet. I didn't know what to do. Then there was Rie—which reminds me, I forgot to tell you about Rie. She was eleven years old and I lived with her. I realized she and the girl who worked at the ropeway would be worried about me, and there wasn't a thing I could do about it. Now the tears began to well up.

"Blubbering won't help, but what the heck. Fate brought you here for some reason. I'll look after you for a while, and maybe we'll think of something. Hey, we're almost there. We'll get lots to eat. More than five puny sardines. We're going to have cream stew with meat in it! So dry your tears, buddy, it's cream stew day!"

I lifted my soggy eyes, and could see that we were at the main gate of an elementary school.

Chapter 6

Cream Stew and Education

Hiding in the bushes, Ippai Attena and I circled the schoolyard, where little kids were doing exercises, and went around to the back. The school building was L-shaped and we had just reached the corner when my sinking heart was suddenly lifted. I'd just finished off a feast of dried sardines, but my appetite was quickly revived by a wonderful smell. It was cream stew.

I'd had it before. Rie's mother always set aside a dish for me, and I loved that thick, rich sauce. Mom knew I didn't eat vegetables, so she just served up the meat—no potatoes or carrots. If she left a bit of carrot, I pushed it aside, but not before licking off the creamy sauce.

Rie and her mother and father had their meals at a table, and I ate underneath it. Rie didn't like carrots either, but she got in trouble for not eating them, so she snuck them into my bowl when her parents weren't looking. Whenever her mother caught her doing this, she said, "Rie, you've got to eat your carrots! You know Rudolf doesn't like them."

Then Rie would sigh and say, "I wish I were a cat. Nobody cares if they don't eat their vegetables."

There were other times she seemed jealous of me too. Like when she had homework. "Cats are lucky. No homework." Or in the morning. "Cats don't have to go to school, why do I have to?"

I wondered just how boring school was, so once I followed her—making sure she didn't notice. She walked with her friends, and it looked to me like they were having fun chatting together. I couldn't figure out why she didn't want to go. I never followed her all the way, so it was news to me that they got to eat cream stew there. Why wouldn't she want to go to school if that's what she got for lunch?

Ippai Attena and I headed directly toward the aroma. We turned a corner to find a corridor connected to another small building. The window was open and two ladies, one thin and one plump, were looking out. When we got closer, we could hear them talking.

"See? I told you he always shows up on stew days."

"How does he know?"

"Beats me!"

I figured they were talking about Ippai Attena. When we got right under the window, the thin lady called out, "Boss, come around to the back!" Just then the plump lady seemed to notice me.

"Goodness me, today he's got a little runt tagging along. It's black. A black cat! Bad luck!"

How rude, I thought. Folks like this are everywhere.

They say black cats bring bad luck. I had no idea why, but I'd heard this saying lots of times. Did they feel that way because I was black? Or because I was a cat? Nobody ever says calico cats are bad luck, so I suppose it's the color. But not everything is trouble because it's black. There're lots of black cars. Guys wear black shoes. Here in Japan, most humans have black hair, too. Take that lady who just said I was bad luck: her hair was black. She should be talking about what bad luck she is every time she looks in a mirror! It's not my fault I was born a cat, and I'm proud of my black fur!

The thin lady came to my rescue.

"There's nothing wrong with black cats. Look at him! He's awfully cute. Come over here, Blacky. Come here, shrimp."

All right already! I was glad she thought I was cute, but my name is Rudolf, I thought, and I wished she would call me that! Of course, we'd just met, so I understood the problem.

"If you say so," said the plump lady. "But I really don't like 'em." I glared at her, but Ippai Attena scolded me.

"Drop it, squirt. It's just a superstition. Anyone who believes it obviously lacks education. She's always saying things like that, but she's not a bad sort."

I didn't know what this "education" was he was talking about. So I asked.

"What's edu . . . edu . . . ?"

"If you have to ask, you don't have it!" Ippai Attena declared. "And you don't have it if you don't know the name of the town you're from."

I still wasn't sure whether or not I had edu . . . whatever it was. And I sure didn't want to be lumped with that bad-luck lady.

"Hold your temper," Ippai Attena said. "Tokyoites talk like that all the time."

Now, what was a Tokyoite? I wanted to ask, but didn't because I didn't want to be accused of not having edu . . . edu . . . just forget it.

"Shut up, and come around to the back. This is where they make lunches. Stay as grumpy as you like, but let's eat!"

So I followed. When we got to the back door, the thin lady was waiting with a plastic bowl of stew. She put it down and squatted down next to us.

"I had no idea you had friends, Boss. There's enough for two here, so be nice and share."

The stew sure looked good, but the bowl wasn't clean. Oh well, I couldn't complain since I was eating out. Ippai Attena and I both shoved our heads in the bowl and licked the stew and chewed up the meat. Cream stew was good wherever you ate it. The flavor was the same whether or not you had edu . . . you know what I mean.

Chapter 7

The Fish Shop and Ippai Attena

That was how my life in Tokyo began. The first week, I stuck close to Ippai Attena. Following him around meant getting lots of good food. Most of it was leftovers from what humans ate. A few times we got dried fish and bonito flakes that weren't leftovers. It turned out that the two women in the school kitchen and the witch lady were not Ippai Attena's only friends. In fact, he visited just about every house in the neighborhood. Then there was the local police officer who shared his lunch with my pal.

One night—the third night after I got to Tokyo—Ippai Attena had been showing me around the neighborhood all day, and I was exhausted. It was late, and the shops were getting ready to close.

"Rudy, didn't you have a fight with your local fishmonger?" said Ippai Attena.

"Yeah, I love fish, but I hate the guys who run those shops. There're a couple near where I live, but both the owners have their eye out for me. I can just be walking by, and they start throwing things."

"Hmm, I wonder if the same thing'd happen here?"

Ippai Attena had a mischievous grin on his face. I rolled my eyes.

"What kind of question is that?" I asked. "Of course it would."

"But you never know unless you try, eh? There's a fish shop over there. Let's walk by and see what happens."

It sounded like a bad idea to me. A cat had no business in front of a fish shop unless he wanted fish.

"I don't wanna do it," I said, but Ippai Attena was already on his way, and I could see the fish shop a few doors away.

A young man in long rubber boots was washing the tiled floor with a pole with a scrubber on the end of it. He didn't seem to notice us. Ippai Attena moved closer—he was right in front of the shop. I decided to stay in front of the vegetable shop next door and watch to see what happened.

Ippai Attena sat down. The man was humming to himself, and his back was to my buddy as he scrubbed the floor. All he had to do was turn around, and it would all be over. Ippai Attena would never be able to dodge that pole. The man was scrubbing backwards, heading to the front of the shop. He got closer and closer to Ippai Attena. When he was no more than a few steps away, I opened my mouth to screech, "Watch out!" but before I could, Ippai Attena meowed.

He was a goner, I knew it. The fishmonger turned

around to look. I shut my eyes.

Well if it's not that thieving cat. I waited for the words I knew were coming—but I was wrong.

"Don't startle me like that, Big Guy," the man chided in a gentle voice, "Move, wouldja, so I can get my work done?"

I couldn't believe my ears. No one would ever be that nice to a cat unless they owned it. And I knew Ippai Attena didn't live there—even though he acted like he did. Ippai Attena moved ever so slightly to the side and beckoned me over. I still wasn't sure, but I obeyed.

"What's going on?" I whispered.

"See for yourself. Nothing's being thrown at us." Sure enough, there we were, sitting in front of the shop, and the owner was still humming and scrubbing.

"Let's go," I pleaded. But just then the fishmonger spoke.

"OK, now I'm done. Let's see what we've got here," and he looked over at us. "Big Guy, is this your kitten? Doesn't look anything like you. Completely black. Anyway, you two wait here a sec."

Did he think Ippai Attena was my father? The man walked back into the shop. Before long he came back out again with two fish.

"These won't keep till tomorrow, and I don't sell rotten fish. You two can have 'em." So saying, the very kind shop owner tossed us the treats.

Ippai Attena thanked him with a very sweet "meow." I decided to play the role of kitten with an even sweeter "meee-ooow" of my own.

Satisfied, the man sent us off. "Right, you guys head home, it's time to close up here."

We picked up our fish in our mouths and trotted off.

So Ippai Attena was friends with the fishmonger, too.

Chapter 8

Education

At night, we slept under the floor boards of the neighborhood shrine. In the dark, Ippai Attena and I talked about lots of different things. I told him about the town I came from, about Rie and the ropeway girl, and about what I could see from the top of the mountain. It made me sad to think about it all, but I wanted to tell my new friend about myself. And I wanted to learn more about him, too. One night I asked Ippai Attena a question that had been on my mind since I'd met him.

"Why do humans call you by all those different names?"

"Well, let me ask you a question. Did you name yourself Rudolf?"

"No, Rie's dad named me. He said it was the name of a king seven hundred years ago. Pretty cool, huh?"

"The name of a king? Must be Rudolf I of Habsburg."

"Whaddaya mean, hab . . . hab . . . ?"

"The Habsburgs were a German family with great power . . . anyway, we can talk about that later. What I mean is, look at me, Rudy. I'm not a king. I'm, well, a stray. And as you can see, I have, uh, connections with many different people. But they don't know each other, right? None of them know what the others call me, so they all give me different names. That old lady you thought was a witch calls me Tiger. The cooks at the school named me Boss. The fishmonger calls me Big Guy, and to the cop at the police box, I'm Bandit. Tiger, Boss, Big Guy, Bandit—they're all my names. That first time I met you and you asked me my name, I said "My name is . . . *ippai attena*—it means 'well, there're a lot of them.'" You thought I was telling you what my name was. You thought I was Ippai Attena. I was just trying to tell you I have many different names—depending on who I'm talking to."

"Yeah, right. Hey, wait a minute, now that you mention it, since I've been here, I've got a bunch of new names: Blacky, Shrimp . . . I get it . . . the more people you know, the more names you have."

Then I asked him why he knew so many people even though he was a stray.

"Look, you have an owner, so you don't know how hard it is to be a stray. We have to work to stay alive. It's either play nice to people or spend all day searching garbage cans. Who wants to live on rotten fish? If you want to eat well, you've got to get along with the humans. It's the only way—other than hunting birds and mice. That's not bad, either, but I like a little variety, you know?"

It was beginning to make sense, but I still had a few questions.

"Ippai Attena, where did you learn to get along so well with people? Did you use to have an owner? A long, long time ago?"

Ippai Attena frowned and turned away.

"You talk too much, Shrimp," he grumped and flopped down on his side and went to sleep.

Touchy subject, I guessed. A few nights later, I asked him something else.

"When we're out walking, I see other cats, but they're always running away or hiding. Why are they so scared of you?"

"I can't be nice to everybody. We strays have to pick and choose to get on in life. You trying smiling and doing that 'mee-ooow' business with everyone. You won't have a thing left to eat. We have to stay on the offensive, snatching food from other cats to keep from starving."

"So why are you so nice to me?"

And once again, the big cat frowned and growled.

"You don't know when to shut up, do you?" he said, flipped over on his side and went to sleep.

I finally figured it out. Everyone has things they don't want to talk about. If anyone ever asked me where I came from, who my owner was, and why I was in Tokyo, I'd start thinking about Rie, and the girl from the ropeway, and the scenery from the mountain top. It'd make me sad if I thought I might never go back there again, and I'd shed a tear or two.

When I talked about this to Ippai Attena, he smiled and said, "You're learning, buddy! That's the start of what they call an education."

Chapter 9

Milk and the Blurry Moon

I arrived in Tokyo right about the time the cherry blossoms began to wilt. Two weeks passed, and then three. I still didn't have a clue about how to get home, but I was getting used to the stray-cat lifestyle. It was even fun sometimes. Or so I told myself. The truth was that I was terribly homesick, but since I didn't have a choice, I decided to make the most of my situation.

Of course, I learned a lot about survival from Ippai Attena. He took me to all the places that fed him, and after a while, I managed to get food even if I went by myself. He taught me to only take what the humans gave me. He said I should never try to get any more than that. He also told me never to go to the same house too often. Once I got food at a certain house, I was supposed to wait two or three days before I went back. Ippai Attena said that cats who went day after day looked cheeky and humans would stop feeding them altogether.

I did everything just the way he taught me. He was older and more experienced at being a stray, so I figured that was the best thing to do. He also showed me that the witch lady was really a very kind old woman.

Once while I was out for a walk, I got stuck in the rain and took shelter under her eaves. But the rain got stronger and I got soaked. I started to worry I might catch cold. Ippai Attena was always telling me that strays had to be careful not to get sick. Cats with owners got taken to the vet, but not strays. Even a simple cold could be dangerous.

So there I was, wet as a dishrag. I was thinking about making a dash for our home under the shrine. But before I ran off, I decided to shake off some of the rain. Just then, the old lady's wooden door opened with a bang.

"Well, if it isn't Blacky. I thought I heard someone out here. You poor thing, you're sopping wet."

Since I've been here, most people call me Blacky. Ippai Attena had lots of names, but I was usually Blacky—or Shrimp. To get back to my story, the old lady picked me up and took me inside. She got a towel out of a chest, put it over my head and started wiping me off all over. It hurt a little, but I figured it would save me catching a cold.

After I was dry, the woman said, "Wait here while I get you some milk." She came back with a saucer and a carton of milk. I love milk. I realized I hadn't had any since I'd been in Tokyo. Rie used to share hers with me all the time. I was so happy I couldn't wait for the old lady to pour it. I stuck my head in the saucer and started drinking it as it came out of the carton and I got some of the milk on my head.

"No need to be in such a rush," the woman said. "No one else is going to drink it. Hold on there! You'll choke. Come on, slow down and drink."

Finally, I was dry and I was full. All I could do now was give a huge yawn. "Sleepy now?" she asked me. "You might as well stay and nap until the rain lets up."

That was just what I was thinking. I found a nice spot in the kitchen.

Far off I thought I heard a familiar voice. It was calling me: "Rudolf, Rudolf, Ruuuudolf!" It was Rie's voice. I tried to answer. I opened my mouth to say "Meow!" but nothing came out. I tried again and again. I wanted to say, *Rie, here I am!* But my voice was gone and I couldn't even move.

"Meow!" Finally!

"Are you awake? You were growling in your sleep and I was about to wake you up. You must have had a bad dream. Was there a dog chasing you?"

The voice wasn't Rie's. It was the old lady's. I'd been having a dream. Now I was really sad. I was still foggy from my nap, but I felt homesick. I was sure I'd stay in Tokyo for the rest of my life and never see my home again.

"Were you someone's cat? What happened? Did you get lost? You can live here if you like. I could keep one little cat like you," said the old lady stroking my back.

She was sweet, but I couldn't stay here when Rie might still be waiting at home for me. I stood up and headed for the door.

"So that's how it is, eh? All right then, you can go now, but come back again. I'll always have milk for you."

The woman opened the door for me, and I could see that the rain had let up and the moon was out. I looked up at it, but my eyes were filled with tears and they made the moon look kind of blurry.

Chapter 10

What Butchy Had to Say

Before I knew it, it was June. Ippai Attena was staying out till late at night. Once I didn't see him for three whole days. I was used to living in Tokyo now, so I was all right on my own, but three days would make anyone anxious.

I wondered if Rie was worried about me. Once when I was still at home, I was out having fun till late. I remember she waited outside for me. I ran to her when I saw her and she ran to me, too. She picked me up and rubbed her face against mine.

"Rudy, you just can't stay out like that," she scolded and took me inside. Did she wait for me like that the first night I was gone? Was she still waiting? Or had she already forgotten me?

Anyway, we were having great weather in Tokyo, and that day, Ippai Attena told me the rainy season would start soon, so I'd better play outside while I could. He said once it started raining he wouldn't be able to get out and about much either, and he had left home early.

It was Sunday. The shrine we lived under had a small park for children, so there were lots of kids out playing—they were so noisy! I decided to go out for a walk and some peace and quiet.

My destination was the elementary school. It was Sunday and I knew no one would be there. I thought I'd go try and catch a sparrow. The short cut to the school went through the shopping street in town, but it was bound to be crowded today, so I took a less busy street that ran parallel to it. The trees in the yards had sprouted leaves, and the sun was shining through them. It was going to be hot, I thought, and looked up at the sky. Just then I heard a voice from above.

"Hey, Rudolf!" I looked in the direction the voice came from. There was a pine tree, but I didn't see anyone. "Over here!" the voice called out.

Again, just a voice. I almost wondered if the tree was talking to me. I went closer. There wasn't a hint of a breeze, but one of the branches was swaying. That must be where the voice was coming from. I stared at the branch a little longer, and sure enough, there was a black-and-white tabby cat. He was perched on the branch and staring down at me.

"Pssst, Rudolf! Are you alone?"

"Yeah."

"You're telling the truth, right? That big lunk you walk around with isn't hiding somewhere?"

"No, it's just me. What's your problem with Ippai Attena?"

"Ippai Attena? Is that what you call him? Whaddaya

know. Around here we call him Stripes, but that's neither here nor there. I'm coming down, so wait a sec, will ya?" The tabby made his way down by climbing from one branch to the next.

"Your name is Rudolf, isn't it?" he asked after he was down on the ground. Now that he mentioned it, how did he know who I was? He also seemed to be able to read my mind, because his next remark was, "You're probably wondering why I know your name. Well, anyone who hangs out with Stripes is bound to become famous. I'm Butchy. You know the hardware shop across from the fish place? I'm their cat."

And what could this hardware shop cat have to do with me? He didn't look very tough, so I figured he wasn't looking for a fight.

"Whaddaya want?" I asked impatiently.

"Nothing, just wanted to chat, you know? Not like I can do that when Stripes is around."

"Why not?"

"I mean there's no right or wrong, it's more like, well, he won't let me."

"You afraid of him?"

"What kinda question is that? Like asking me if the sun rises in the east."

"So you are."

"Everyone is. The only one who isn't is Devil, the Ogawa's pet."

I had to admit I didn't hate it when everyone said they were terrified of Ippai Attena. On the one hand, I wondered why he couldn't be friends with the others. But on the other hand it was kind of cool to be the only one he was nice to. What bugged me now was that there was a cat who wasn't afraid of him.

"So what sort of cat is this Devil anyway?" I tried not to sound like I cared.

"He's not a cat," Butchy replied. "Stripes wouldn't let a cat get away with anything. Devil's a dog, a bulldog, for your information."

Huh, a dog. That was a relief. I knew Ippai Attena had to be the toughest cat around. I nodded—like it was exactly what I expected.

"If Devil were a normal dog," Butchy went on, "it wouldn't matter—dogs are no different from cats. I've seen Stripes fight off a stray dog before. What a sight. After that, you wouldn't catch anyone talking about whether he was strong or not."

I wanted to hear more, and Butchy was ready to accommodate.

"It's hot out here in the sun. How about taking this conversation into a cooler spot in that pine over there?"

Ippai Attena was always telling me not to follow any old cat. You never knew what kind of trap they had laid. I hesitated to follow Butchy up into that tree; there might be some other cat there. Butchy noticed.

"Stop worrying," he said. "I won't touch you. None of us cats would. I mean, it'd be fine if you nailed me, but what if I accidentally got a few punches in? I hate to think about what Stripes would do to me." He began climbing the tree, and I followed.

It was cool up in the pine, and there was a good view. I loved tree climbing: you could go so high. I caught up with Butchy partway and just kept going.

"Hey," he called, "stop where you are. You wanna fall?" I wanted to keep going, but I also wanted to hear what Butchy had to say. So I decided to stop and wait for him. "Man, it's dangerous way up here," he panted. "How d'ya plan to get down?"

That's what he said, but he smiled as he looked out at the view. There was a good spot with two branches growing out of the trunk, and we settled on them.

"So," I said, picking up where we'd left off, "what happened when Ippai Attena fought that stray dog?"

"Right, right. Well, it was something. He batted at him once and that was the end of it."

"There's got to be more to the story than that."

"Calm down, and let me talk." Butchy finally got down to the interesting parts. "When was it, hmm? Ah yes, last winter. I was taking a nap in a pool of sunlight, when I heard a lot of noise in the back of the house. There was a growl and then a *scre-e-e-ech*. The screech was Stripes. I sound like him, right? And then a growl, *rrr-r-*

r-r-r. That was the dog. I can never get that one down. More like a *rooof-f-f* than an *rrr-r-r-r* maybe. Wait, wait, more like *RRR-R-gruff*. Or was it *GR-r-r-r-uffff*? No, definitely *RRR-R-gruff*."

"Whatever," I said, anxious to hear what happened next. "Who cares if it was *rrr-r-r-r-r* or *gr-R-R-R-uffff*?"

"That's not what I said," Butchy seemed determined to set the record straight. "It was *RRR-R-gruff*."

"Get on with it, will ya?"

"Sound effects are important to a narrative, but if you insist. The dog and the cat were growling and howling, trying to scare each other off. I jumped up and ran to the window. I pushed my head under the curtain and looked out. Stripes and that dog were raring to go. The dog wasn't local; he'd just ended up here. He was, let me see, brown and twice as big as Stripes—well, almost twice as big. He had a scar on his forehead and was a nasty piece of work. Always chasing cats around. Me too once. I managed to climb a tree and save myself. Dogs don't climb trees, you know. But that dimwitted mutt hung around for a while and barked at me. Dogs know they can't climb, but it would be bad form not to bark for a while, I guess. All I can say is, it was *terrifying*!" I leaned forward as I listened and almost fell out of the tree. "Watch out there, friend!" warned Butchy. "So, as I was saying, that dog was a nasty piece of work.

"That day, he came closer to Stripes and started

barking his head off. Stripes hunkered down, and snarled back. A second later, the dog made a move, but Stripes was one-hundredth of a second quicker! He knew where that dog was heading and jumped at a diagonal, and came down right on that dog's dirty nose with his left paw. And he didn't stop there. He flipped around in mid-air and came down on the dog's back. He dug his left front claws into its nose and his right front claws into its forehead, and then bit the dog right in the ear."

"Hold on a sec," I interrupted. "Wouldn't it have been better to go for the dog's eyes with his claws?"

Butchy must have been waiting for that, because he eagerly began explaining.

"That just proves that Stripes is smarter than the rest of us. Anyone else would have gone for the eyes, but not him. If he had done that, the dog would've gone blind for sure. He was a stray, right? Without his vision, how could he've survived? Dogs are dogs and cats are cats, but strays are all strays. Stripes always keeps that sort of thing in mind."

That's when I finally realized just how wise Ippai Attena really was. But Butchy wasn't finished with his story.

"I was at the part where Stripes bit into the dog's ear, right? Well once you've bitten down, you're not going to give up, you know? Stripes kept his teeth in the dog's ear and his claws in the dog's nose and forehead. It must've been unbearable. That mutt started yelping and Stripes jumped off its back.

"'You're hardly worth the breath,' Stripes snarled, 'but I'm warning you not to come back around here. Next time I'll bite off both your ears, and you'll look like a rat in a ski cap!' That's what he said! I swear. It was very cool."

It was hard to tell whether Butchy was impressed with Ippai Attena or just with his own storytelling. I was feeling pretty impressed myself with my good friend's victory. When he was done, Butchy and I just sat there for a while thinking about it all.

Finally, Butchy spoke up. "Whoops, got to go! Can't be late for lunch!" And he began to hustle down the tree. I sat there for a while longer thinking about Ippai Attena.

"You're hardly worth the breath, but I'm warning you not to come back around here. Next time I'll bite off both your ears, and you'll look like a rat in a ski cap!" I said the same line to see how it sounded. It was cool no matter who said it, I decided.

Next I tried a lower, huskier voice. Even better. As I practiced sounding tough, like Ippai Attena, Butchy made his way down the tree. When he reached the bottom, he called back up to me.

"Hey, Rudolf! I'm off. You be careful coming down, you hear? And let me tell you one more thing: Stripes used to have a human owner. See you!"

I just kept on practicing that line. "You're hardly

worth the breath, but . . . wait, hey, did you say something?"

Butchy turned around once more.

"And another thing. He can read human writing. Incredible, right? OK then, catch you later!"

I was barely listening. I just kept on practicing as I watched him go.

You'll look like a rat in a ski cap! Just then, I heard something up in the branches over my head. A pigeon had landed at the very top of the tree. I tried out my line again.

"Yeah, you pigeon! You're hardly worth the breath, but I'm warning you not to come back around here. Next time I'll bite off both your ears, and you'll look like a rat in a ski cap!" I glared at the bird and realized that he didn't have any ears to start out with.

The pigeon cooed loudly and flew off. I was a little embarrassed but kept up the tough attitude. "Heh! Showed you!" I wasn't sure who had shown who, but I said it anyway.

It was time to climb down, and just as I was about to do so, I suddenly remembered what Butchy said as he walked off. Had he . . . ? Yes, he had! He said Ippai Attena used to have owners—he was kept by humans, and he could read human writing. In a moment of amazement, my feet slipped and I fell out of the tree, landing hard on my back.

Chapter 11

Ippai Attena Gets Angry

Fortunately, I wasn't injured. I'd hate to be known as the cat who got hurt falling out of a tree. We're supposed to be able to flip around in the air and land on both feet. My back hurt, but I managed to pull myself up, and looked around to make sure no one was watching.

I didn't see anyone, so I tried to look like nothing was wrong and marched off from under the pine tree. When I got to the main gate of the school, I crawled under it and into the playground. As expected, the place was deserted. Along the concrete block wall between the playground and the road was a line of trees. Small thin trees alternated with larger ones in a zigzag pattern. I hid up in a bigger tree and waited for sparrows.

There was only one thing I was better at than Ippai Attena: catching sparrows. It might have been different if he'd really tried, but he didn't seem particularly interested in the birds. There are two kinds of cats: rat catchers and bird catchers. Ones who like rats are called mousers, and ones like me are called birders. I learned that from Ippai Attena. He told me he was more of a mouser.

If you don't know about catching birds, you might

think all you have to do is hide in a high place and attack anything you see moving below. But it's not that easy.

First of all, sparrows are sensitive to anything bigger and higher up than they are—and not just sparrows, cats are the same really. Bigger animals are bound to be stronger, so you've just got to pay attention when they're around. If your enemy is the same size as you, then being higher up is an advantage. And you sure don't want to be lower than your enemy. That's why you've got to be aware of anything up above.

Then there's another reason why it's hard to catch a sparrow when it's on the ground. It has to do with timing. When a sparrow takes off, it uses its wings and its legs too. Let me explain. At the same time it spreads its wings, a sparrow jumps with its legs. A solid, stable spot is easier to jump from than anything that moves. It's the same whether you're a cat or a human, or a bird. Try it sometime! It takes an instant longer to leap off of a tree branch than to jump on the ground. And that tiny instant is the difference between victory and defeat.

I always try to hunt sparrows in trees on tiny branches that are higher than my vantage point. I settle on the branch of a big tree, and wait for sparrows to light on the branches of smaller trees. I pounce on them and knock them off with my front legs. You may think it's violent and cruel, but it's all part of survival for us animals. Sparrows catch worms and humans catch fish to eat.

Don't try telling me you've never had meat or fish!

Anyway, that's why the trees in the playground were great places for catching birds. So there I was. I'd crawled under the gate, and was walking over to the trees, when I happened to see a cat sitting in the sand under the horizontal bars. His back was to me, but I could tell right away it was Ippai Attena.

"Hey! Ippai Attena!" I called out, and ran over to the sandbox. When I got closer, my pal turned his head to look at me.

"Well, if it isn't Rudy. Sparrow hunting again?"

"Right!" I was glad to see him, because I wanted to practice my new line on him. "By the way, does this sound familiar?" I switched to a rough, gravelly voice, and said, "You're hardly worth the breath, but I'm warning you not to come back around here. Next time I'll bite off both your ears, and you'll look like a rat in a ski cap."

I was just finishing up when Ippai Attena's paw whipped out and caught me in the head. Whap! It knocked me over. I was too shocked to say anything.

"Wh-wh-what's that for?" I finally managed.

"Whaddaya mean what's that for? Where did you hear that?" demanded Ippai Attena, and he was angry.

"Did you think I was gonna bite off your ears? I was just telling you what you said!"

"Yeah, I figured that out. I wanna know where you

heard it!"

"Where? What's it matter, I mean . . . nowhere." My voice cracked, but I tried to hold back the tears. He'd never hit me before.

"It was that Butchy from the hardware shop, wasn't it? He tells everyone."

"I'm not supposed to talk to Butchy from the hardware shop? I can talk to whoever I want!" Now I was in pain *and* angry.

Ippai Attena looked sad when I said that.

"Nobody's saying you can't talk to Butchy. And I'm sorry I hit you. Did it hurt? Look, Rudy. I was wrong to do that. But, well, why don't you sit down here."

My head smarted, but I sat down on the sand.

"Rudolf, I've been meaning to talk to you about this for a while. You've got a smart mouth. It's because you hang out with me all the time, so it's partly my fault. But just because I say something doesn't mean you can mimic it. When you talk tough and sound nasty, your mind starts thinking it's tough and that it's acceptable to be mean. When you're a stray, I know you can't act all high and mighty and sophisticated. But you plan to go home one day, don't you? You want to live with your human family, right? Do you think Rie is going to be happy to see you acting like this? Think about it."

It was bad enough getting knocked down by Ippai Attena. Now he'd gone and started talking about Rie. I could feel the tears welling up.

Suddenly I remembered how Rie's mother used to pick me up and say, "A very classy cat we have!" Had I really started sounding crass? I had to admit, I wasn't talking the way I used to. I didn't have a word to say in my own defense, so Ippai Attena kept talking.

"And another thing. That was a special line for a particular occasion where I really needed to get a point across. You can't just say it whenever you feel like it. I was fighting a dog. That dog wasn't living as a stray to pass the time, ya know?"

I just nodded. "As long as you understand," Ippai Attena said. "And I'm sorry I hit you."

Now that he'd mentioned the stray dog, I remembered that I had a question for him.

"Do you mind if I ask you about something else? Is it true that you used to be kept by humans? And that you can read?"

Ippai Attena turned back to glare at me again. I was pretty sure I'd made another mistake.

Chapter 12

Ippai Attena's Secret

Ippai Attena looked at me angrily for a few seconds. Then he seemed to think better of it, and sighed.

"Did Butchy tell you that too?"

I didn't say anything. Even if Ippai Attena knew Butchy had told me, I certainly wasn't going to mention his name. Finally he said, "Well, it doesn't really matter who said it." He looked up at the June sky. The sun was bright, and the temperature was rising. Sitting there in the sandbox, my back was starting to heat up. There's a saying that there are only three days a year when it's too hot for a cat, but that's a lie. Hot days are better than cold, but we cats get plenty hot in the summer.

Even if Ippai Attena refused to answer me, I knew now that he used to belong to someone. His silence was all the proof I needed. I also knew it was a question that, for some reason, I shouldn't have asked. Who knows? Maybe it made him sad to think about it.

"I'm sorry, Ippai Attena," I apologized, "I didn't mean to hurt you. I just keep making you mad." I decided to go somewhere else for the day. It wasn't because I didn't want to get in trouble again. I just didn't want to see him so sad. "I'm going to go catch some sparrows. I'll get some for you too."

"Forget the sparrows for now," Ippai Attena said as I stood up. "Come sit down over here. I was going to have to tell you someday. It might as well be now. It's true. I used to live with humans. Do you remember that house with a big gingko tree over by the shops?"

The house where the bulldog lives, I thought. The one Butchy told me about. It had to be. Now that he mentioned it, I realized Ippai Attena hardly ever went around there. It must be because of that terrifying dog named Devil. I'd seen him once from up on the fence. He had a huge mouth, like a monster. His lips were black and hung in flaps. His body reminded me of a cardboard box with four hams stuck into it. He was a light brown and his eyes looked greedy. I could tell he was a nasty piece of work.

"I know the place," I answered. "Doesn't the Ogawa family live there?"

"Exactly. There's a vacant lot next to the Ogawas. There used to be a house there, and I lived in it."

It was a big lot, so it must have had a big house on it.

"What happened?" I asked.

"Moved away."

"Where?"

"Far away."

"How far?"

"Farther away than the town you came from."

"How do you know that?"

Ippai Attena got a faraway look on his face.

"Left Japan entirely," he said softly. Now I was confused.

"Look Rudy, you came in a truck, right? My human went somewhere you can't reach in a truck. You've got to take a plane."

I knew what airplanes were. They flew overhead and made loud sounds. But I didn't know humans rode in them.

"You don't say."

"There's a big river a little ways from here," said Ippai Attena, and I knew the one he meant. I'd been there just once. There was a river like that in the town I used to live in. Looking at it made me feel homesick, so I never went back. "That river goes on and on until it reaches the sea," my friend continued.

I'd never seen the sea before, but Ippai Attena had told me about it. He said it was like an endless pond. It was thousands of times deeper than a pond, and wider too. In a storm, there would be waves that were dozens of meters tall. Fish and other creatures lived in the water. One was called a whale and it was bigger than a human or even a tiger—even a truck. It was the biggest living creature on earth. Ippai Attena told me all this—he knew everything.

"The river goes on until it reaches Tokyo Bay," my pal kept on talking.

"What's that?" Things were starting to get confusing now.

"Tokyo Bay is like a big cove. Once you leave it, you're in the Pacific Ocean, the biggest sea in the world. Beyond that is North America. It's a big continent, lots bigger than Japan. That's where my human went—to a country in North America called the United States."

It was all too big for me, and I was completely lost. All I knew was that Ippai Attena's human was in a gigantic place that was incredibly far away. Maybe farther away than the moon. I thought I'd ask him if the United States was that far, but I'd been in enough trouble for one day, so I kept quiet.

"Just to be clear, I didn't have a family like you did. There were no children, just one adult man. He lived in a big house all by himself. One day, five years ago, he called me and said, 'Tiger, we can't live together anymore. And you can't stay here, because this house is going to be torn down. It was never mine to begin with. I just rent. I'm going to the United States by myself. And you're going to have to get by on your own now.'

"Tiger was what he called me. Then one day, he left with all of his things. I stayed there for a while, but then bulldozers and power shovels showed up and tore down the whole place. That's when I made my exit, and I've lived as a stray ever since."

I listened quietly. Ippai Attena had a nostalgic look on his face, so I just let him talk.

"My human was an interesting guy. He'd come home every night, have a glass of whiskey and tell me stories. Then one night he said—I have no idea why—'Tiger, I'm going to start teaching you to read.' I didn't really want to, but he grabbed me and put a rope around my neck to keep me from escaping. Then he got out a children's drawing pad and drew one character on each page. He wrote them really big. He said, 'this is あ,' 'this is い.' Like that. For the next ten days he taught me the first five hiragana characters. Over and over and over. I didn't have any choice but to learn.

"Every once in a while, he'd say, 'I wonder if you really understand,' but he never quit trying. Then he went onto the other hiragana, and it lasted maybe two months. You've got to give him credit for trying. I mean there was no way he could tell whether I really learned what he was teaching me. He just decided how long he thought it should take. And I've got to say, I'm a smart cat. He taught me for two months, but I had most of them learned in the first month. After hiragana, he taught me katakana. That took another two months. Then he started teaching me some simple kanji characters. He taught me every night for a year. Maybe thirty minutes a day. And he wouldn't let me outside until we were done. After a year, I could read a newspaper. It was a lot of work, but now I'm glad I did it."

"Is it useful to know how to read human writing?" I finally spoke up.

"It is! I never could have imagined how useful it could be while I was learning it. What I still don't understand is why he taught me in the first place." Ippai Attena stopped to think, and I took the opportunity to speak again.

"So, how do you use it?"

"For different things. I mean, I bring you to the school lunch kitchen, right? And every time they're making cream stew. What about when you go alone? You told me they were making curry and you couldn't eat any of it. So why do you think they have stew when we go together, but curry when you go alone?"

Now that he mentioned it, the other day I'd asked him if he wanted to go to school for lunch, and he told me they weren't having cream stew and turned me down. He knew what they were having without having to go find out.

"I go in the evenings and look in the window. There's a blackboard on the wall, and they write the menu for the whole week on it. If you can read, you know what they're having and when."

"So that's how you know." I was dumbfounded. "Is there anything else you can do if you read?" My head was full of questions.

"Yes, Rudy. Lots of things. I know about North America and the United States. I know about animals besides cats and dogs—all those things I tell you about." It was true. I was always surprised at how much he knew. "My human told me some things, but the other stuff I read about in books."

"Book? What's a book?"

"It's easier to show you one than try to explain it." Ippai Attena got up and headed towards the school building.

Chapter 13

School Books and Education

The school was closed because it was Sunday. Once I'd thought I'd take a walk through the school on a weekend and looked for a place to get in. The entrance was shut, so I had given up.

Ippai Attena didn't give up, though. He went around the back. The three-story classroom building had three rows of windows, one on each floor. Below some of the big windows, there were some small, thin ones. Ippai Attena reached up to one of these windows with his front paws. He hooked a claw on it and pressed against it with his paw. I heard a creaky noise and the window opened a crack. He stuck his head through the opening and wagged it back and forth so the window was finally open wide enough for us to get through. Ippai Attena pulled up his back feet and slipped through the window. I followed.

We found ourselves in a long hallway, along which there was one classroom after another. What was he planning to do, I wondered. The classroom doors were heavy; there was no way we could open them. But there were little windows between the hallway and the classrooms, just like the one we had climbed through to get inside.

"Your turn, Rudy," said Ippai Attena. I went over to a window and saw it was low to the floor, so I didn't have to reach far. I put my front paws to it, gave a few good pushes, and it opened. I crawled through first. There were a bunch of desks and chairs inside.

"Hey, look, here we are!" Ippai Attena was over by some bookshelves.

"They're no big deal," I scoffed, "Rie's got them too."

"If you know about them, why didn't you say so?" Ippai Attena sounded irritated.

"Are these the 'books' you were talking about? Don't you call them texts? Rie told me about them."

"Texts are books. But not all books are textbooks. Come take a look." Ippai Attena used his front paw to pull out a big volume with a thick cover off of a shelf. He cleverly used his nose to turn the pages. Inside the book were pictures of different animals.

"This is a tiger, and this one next to it is a lion." On the same page there were lots of animals that looked kind of like cats. "This is called *The Illustrated Book of Animals*. There are lots of pictures, but some books don't have any pictures at all—just words. We can't take out too many at once because it'll look suspicious. We cats can take books off a shelf, but it's hard to get them back on. Let's look at one other book and then call it a day."

Ippai Attena reached for a book on a higher shelf. "Here's one with more words in it. It's what they call a biography. About a guy named Edison."

"Biography?" I'd never heard that word before.

"It means a book about someone's life. If you read it, you'll understand what kind of person this Edison was."

"Do they have a biography of Rie?"

Ippai Attena smirked.

"Biographies are only about famous people."

"What's so famous about the guy, Edi-*san*?"

"Not Edi-*san*, it's EdiSON. But that's not the point. What I want to say is, if you can read, you can find out about everything written here."

"Do you think I can learn how to read if I try?"

"Of course. But you'll really have to work hard—do what they call study. It takes years even for human children to learn how to do it. They have to learn to read and write too. Our paws are different from their hands, so we can't really write very much at once." As he talked, Ippai Attena moved his hand in zigzag motions.

"Teach me how to read!" I jumped up and down in excitement.

"I can teach you, but it's not easy to learn. You can't play all day and learn how to read at the same time."

"I know! I'll do it. Come on, please? I'm a quick learner, really."

"I'll think about it. We've had enough for today. Let's

go home."

I wanted to stay a little longer, but Ippai Attena was in charge. We walked back from the classroom to the hallway, and from the hallway, back outside. Ippai Attena was careful to close the small window we'd crept through.

"Otherwise, they'll figure out cats got inside," he explained, "and then they'll start locking the windows and we'll never get back in."

I knew humans loved locking things. In fact, it was a miracle we were able to open those windows. I asked my friend about it.

"So why aren't there any locks on those windows?"

Ippai Attena laughed.

"Locks and keys are to keep out burglars. No human could ever get through those little windows. As long as they don't have to worry about burglars, there's no need to lock anything. But if they found out cats were in and out all the time, they'd lock the windows to keep us from causing trouble. Then I'd never be able to read books. If you ever come back on your own, don't forget to close up, OK?"

"I'll do my best, Sensei!" I declared. Ippai Attena looked just a little pleased to be called sensei.

"Unless you get a little education—like me—it won't have been worth your time to come to Tokyo. And I've got lots more to learn, too. We looked at the classroom books, but there's a library in there with even more of them. Problem is, they close it up tight on weekends. We won't make our way in there anytime soon. Every once in a while, someone'll forget to close the door. Not often though."

"Why do you still want to learn when you can already read?" I asked.

"There are things I want to do . . . but we don't need to talk about that now." Being able to read seemed like plenty to me, but I didn't push it. I was glad he wasn't irritated at me anymore—and I was determined to become an educated cat.

Chapter 14

Youth Is Wasted on the Young

Time passed quickly when you were focused. I started learning to read the day after we snuck into the school. But first, Ippai Attena made me promise I wouldn't give up partway through.

We set off for school early each morning and got there before the children arrived. The days are long during the summer, so we had lots of time if we left as the sun rose. Ippai Attena taught me how to read in the sandbox under the parallel bars. He drew the characters with his paw in the sand. "This is あ, and this is い," said Ippai Attena starting with the first two characters. He said I wouldn't be able to remember them if he showed me too many at first, so that first day we did あ (a), い (i), and う(u).

Ippai Attenai drew the character, and I did my best to imitate it.

あ

Then he'd draw the next one, and, again, I'd copy him.

い

Then the next one.

う

After I could draw them one at a time, he had me draw them altogether:

あいう

あいう

あいう

Over and over, I practiced. My front paws got completely worn out. They weren't used to this writing business.

The next day, Ippai Attena taught me え (e) and お (o). After that we reviewed what we'd done the day before. That first week, I only learned two or three characters a day. He started moving more quickly from the second week. But after every new thing he taught me, he always went back and reviewed what I'd already learned. It took me all of June to get through the hiragana syllabary.

At first I couldn't tell ぬ (nu) and め (me) apart. Or れ (re) and わ (wa). Even when I made mistakes, though, Ippai Attena never got mad at me. He was actually nicer when I was having a tough time.

"It's the same for everyone at the beginning," he explained. "You'll get better, so don't worry about it!"

Once I'd learned hiragana, the katakana syllabary went a lot faster. By the middle of July, I could read and write both of them. At night, I went out by myself to a nearby park that had a sandbox and was lit up at night, so I could get in some practice.

One night, Butchy showed up.

"Hey Rudolf, whatcha doing there? Digging around in the sand?" I ignored him, but he seemed determined to find out. "You're not a dog, ya know," he continued, "so don't try hiding food there."

"I'm not hiding anything. I'm practicing writing."

"Writing? Well, I'll be. Is Stripes teaching you?"

I just nodded and kept on working. Butchy plopped down behind me and began scratching his neck with his back leg, and yawning. Occasionally, he'd talk and interrupt me.

"So why are you learning to write? No good can come out of cats studying."

When that didn't stop me, he got more blunt.

"Wouldja just stop? You look like a fool. Let's go climb a tree. The higher you get the cooler it is."

I ignored him and kept on writing in the sand, but Butchy refused to give up.

"Whoops, I tripped," he said, spoiling the character I was working on. I moved a little to one side and kept at it. But Butchy continued bothering me.

"Ya know, I think I remember hiding a rat's tail somewhere around here. Let me see, where was it?" He started digging around and spraying me with sand.

Now I was annoyed, so I wrote in the sand ブッチーは、なまけものの、おばかさん (Butchy is a lazy fool). Then I called out to him, "Here, look at this! It says 'Butchy is cute and clever.'" He stopped kicking sand for a moment and came over to take a look.

"Ya don't say! That's how you write 'Butchy is cute and clever!' All right then, next why don't you write, 'Butchy is a good-looking tabby cat.'"

"My pleasure," I said, and wrote out ブッチーは、きたない、ブスねこさん (Butchy is dirty and ugly to boot). I was really having fun and it was all I could do to keep from laughing out loud. Butchy came a little closer and made another request.

"Butchy is a strong, but gentle and active youth. Write that next!"

I wrote ブッチーは、まぬけで、やらしい、がんこなばかもの (Butchy is a clumsy, rude, stubborn nitwit). Finally, I couldn't hold it in anymore and burst out laughing.

"What's so funny?" demanded Butchy. "Ah, I know! You wrote something else, didn't you! What was it?"

I couldn't stop laughing, so I ran off.

"I knew it! Come back here! TELL ME WHAT YOU WROTE!" Butchy took off after me, still screaming. We tore around the little park until he finally caught me and we started wrestling.

"What was it, huh? You better tell me!"

"Ha ha ha! I wrote, 'Butchy is a clumsy, rude, stubborn nitwit.'"

"How dare you! Now you're gonna get it!" He bit down on my tail, right at the root. Now I couldn't stop crying—because I was laughing so hard, and also from the pain. "Ha ha ha, ouch ouch! Ha ha, quit that! Ha ha ha, oh that hurts! Stop it, stop it, oh, ha ha ha!"

There's a saying about youth being wasted on the young, and I'm sure we looked like the most foolish of young cats. There we were flying around the park like we were going to rip each other apart, but we were just having fun.

Chapter 15

Boss and Mr. Bear

"It's summer vacation," said Ippai Attena one muggy night as we were lying on the cool roof tiles of the shrine.

"So? It doesn't mean anything to cats, does it? I mean every day's a holiday for us," I responded. Then I realized what Ippai Attena was talking about. "Oh, that's right! Now those kids will be here every morning, running around playing and shouting!"

"That's true, but it's not what I'm getting at. Think hard now, Rudy," said Ippai Attena. He didn't sound annoyed at all. "Where're kids on school days?"

"What kind of question is that? School, of course."

"So, when school is closed, who's there?" asked Ippai Attena, sounding unusually patient.

"Nobody. It's empty!" And the moment I said it, I knew. Nobody would be at school all summer! I'd be able to practice writing in the sandbox and we could sneak into classrooms. I suddenly had lots of energy, and sat up.

"There you go." Ippai Attena sounded pleased too, and raised his plump body. "While kids are playing, we get to study. They get the shrine, we get the school. But there's one bad thing about summer vacation. Know what it is?"

What could possibly be wrong, I wondered.

"Something's missing when the kids are gone."

"No classes, right?"

"Think again . . . something you like a lot."

"No school lunch, no stew!" I said when it finally hit me. Now that was a problem. "And no meat," I muttered and lay down again. Stray cats beg for food at people's houses or scavenge food from garbage cans. We get a lot of fish, but not much meat. For some reason, when humans think "cats," they immediately think "fish." What was that about?

Next morning, we slept in because we didn't have to go to school so early when no one was there. Unlike on Sundays, the school's main gate was open.

"I thought the school was closed," I said.

"Some teachers come to do a little work," replied Ippai Attena nonchalantly.

"We can't get into the school building then," I grumbled, disappointed.

"Rudolf, you're forgetting something," Ippai Attena smirked. I was in no mood to play guessing games.

"Forget? I'm not like human kids who bring stuff to school. Notebooks and pencils—I don't need them, so I don't forget anything!"

"That's obvious. Never heard of a lost-and-found box for cats, that's for sure. I'm not talking about things, but facts."

"Not things, but facts. What? Come on, you're always talking in riddles. Just give me the answer."

My pal smiled; he seemed determined to draw out this moment. Finally, he spread out his front paws for the announcement.

"A fanfare, please . . . Ta dah! The answer is . . . Mr. Ippai Attena knows a lot of humans and has excellent social skills."

"Wow! Do you know some of the teachers?"

"Bingo! Now let's go." Ippai Attena dashed off toward the school building, and—as usual—I followed.

When we got right outside the faculty room, Ippai Attena looked up at the window and cried *meow*. It was amazing how he could sound so sweet when it came to humans. That's feigned innocence—or maybe you might call it feline innocence. All the faculty room windows were closed. The air conditioning must be on, I thought. Ippai Attena meowed a little louder. The windows stayed shut. Next he tried something a little more aggressive.

"*Meee-OWWW!*"

The window finally creaked open, and a bear looked out. A bear! I loved picture books of animals. Every time I sneaked into the school on Sundays, I read them. I learned the names of almost all the animals because illustrations included their names in katakana. I can read katakana, you know. Anyway, a man with a beard was peeking out the window, and he looked exactly like a big brown bear.

"All right, all right, I hear you! It's just I'm tied up with something." The bear went inside, leaving the window open.

"Let's go." Ippai Attena leaped through it, with me right behind.

There was only one bear—no, one bearlike human—in the faculty room. As we settled ourselves on the windowsill, he scolded us, "Hurry up! You're letting out the cool air."

The bear guy was writing something at his desk by the window. After we jumped in, he closed the window with his left hand, and kept writing with his right. "Cats are lucky, all your time is free time. I've got so many things to do even during summer break," he mumbled to himself.

"Ippai Attena, when did you meet this guy?" I whispered.

"Well, the other day, I went to the kitchen after lunch. I like to vary my times so I don't look too greedy. So I dropped by when the ladies were about finished cleaning up. Found them drinking tea with this teacher and made friends with him. He looked kinda scary, but he seemed nice."

I figured if he looked like an animal, it might make him nicer to other animals. The faculty room was cool and it felt good. I half closed my eyes and twitched my nose. Then, suddenly, Mr. Bear gave a big yawn and stretched.

"Done for the day! Now shall I play with the cats or something?"

What? I thought to myself, now wide awake. Play with the cats or *something*? How rude! I turned to Ippai Attena to urge him to leave, but Ippai Attena had started scratching the door to the hallway.

"Want to go out, huh?" Mr. Bear stood up and opened the door. Ippai Attena went out. I didn't want to be left alone with this guy. It wasn't like I could teach him tricks or anything! I quickly stood up and followed my friend out.

In the hall, Ippai Attena took several steps and stopped. He looked up at Mr. Bear leaning against the doorpost, and meowed. Now what?

"I let you out because you wanted to go. Still got something to complain about?" Mr. Bear said, scratching his bearded cheek. Ippai Attena took a few more steps, halted, and meowed again.

"What? What do you want?" Mr. Bear walked toward Ippai Attena, who took several more steps forward. "Hey, where you going?" Mr. Bear came closer to Ippai Attena, who then took some more steps. "Now what? Where you going?" he asked again. After a few more repetitions of this little act, Mr. Bear finally said, "All right. You want to take me somewhere. Time for a stroll with the kitty cats, I guess."

First it was "cats or something," and now it was "kitty cats." What an oddball! And where was Ippai Attena headed? I was getting tired of the both of them, so I decided to go to a classroom to look at a book on birds. When I turned around and started walking away, Ippai Attena called me from behind.

"Wait, Rudy, where're you off to?"

"Where? It's no fun looking at a cat-and-bear circus show. I'm off to find a book with pictures of sparrows."

"You are a bird brain! There's more than a month of vacation. We've got lots of time to come back and see your fine-feathered friends. Right now you need to come along with us, pronto!"

I didn't know what he was up to. But Ippai Attena was serious, so I decided to follow him and the bear. Now we were a parade of three—a cat that looked like a tiger, a human who looked like a bear, and a furry black ringleader—that was me. Just like a circus troupe.

Chapter 16

The Library and Human Progress

Ippai Attena went up the stairs followed by Mr. Bear, shifting his weight from one foot to the other. I was at the back. When he reached the second floor, Ippai Attena started running.

"No, don't run! No running in the hall," shouted Mr. Bear, trotting behind him. Ippai Attena got on pretty well with humans, and Mr. Bear definitely seemed to understand cats. I was beginning to see why Ippai Attena liked him.

When we arrived at the end of the hallway, Mr. Bear was sweating and panting. "Now it's the library. What business d'you have here?" Ippai Attena started scratching the steel door. "All right, I'll open it for you." Mr. Bear pulled out a bundle of keys from his trouser pocket. He chose one and jabbed it into the keyhole. The key just rattled.

"No, not this one. Maybe this is the right one?"

Rattle, rattle . . .

"No, wrong again. This must be it."

Rattle, rattle . . .

None of the keys fit, and Ippai Attena kept scratching

the door impatiently.

Rattle, rattle . . . scratch . . . rattle . . . scratch . . . scratch.

The sound of claws and wrong keys resonated in the empty hallway.

Click!

"Hurray, this is it!" Mr. Bear said happily. The moment the steel door opened an inch, Ippai Attena dove into the room. I slipped between the bear's legs to follow.

The library was spectacular, with row after row of books neatly stacked on the shelves. A classroom book collection was nothing compared to this. The library itself was twice or three times as large as a classroom. At the center were many big tables. They must have been for children to sit at and read books. Ippai Attena leaped onto a table and looked around. I jumped up and sat beside him.

"Awesome! More books than a bookstore!" I crowed.

"Great, isn't it?" Ippai Attena was as thrilled as I was. "There're lots of picture books, too—the sort you like. Animals, plants, birds, fish. You'll find illustrated books on rocks, stars, and even cars."

"Then I'm gonna look for bird books." I was about to jump off the table, but Ippai Attena grabbed my tail.

"Not now. Just enjoy the view today. He's watching us," said Ippai Attena glancing at Mr. Bear. "Can't let the cat out of the bag. Start reading under his nose, and he'll know who's been into the books in the classrooms." We had a treasure box right in front of our nose, but it was just out of reach.

"What the heck are we here for, then?" I complained.

"Hey kid, you were impressed with teeny little classroom libraries. So I wanted to show you something bigger. And there's a place even better than this, an entire building of books."

"What? A building made of books?"

"No, a big building packed with books."

"Wow . . ." I was amazed at the thought.

"But it's a waste for someone like you who can only read hiragana and katakana."

Now that hurt my pride. I knew about kanji characters and that they were even tougher than hiragana and katakana, but I had thought I could get away without having to learn them. I thought I already knew everything! Ippai Attena cut in on my thoughts.

"Rudy, the other night, you made fun of Butchy because he can't read. Don't do that again. I didn't teach you so that you can rag on others. You've learned a little bit, and now you're stuck up and look down on other cats. Cats with education don't do things like that."

How did Ippai Attena know about that episode the other night? He must have been watching. My heart sank.

"OK, never mind," he went on. "Beginners always

want to show off. Now, let's go. Any longer, and he'll start suspecting us of mischief." I turned to see Mr. Bear. He was leaning against the steel door and yawning.

"Hey, you cats, what business do you have here? I've never heard of cats in a library before. C'mon now."

"See? Humans don't believe cats can improve themselves," Ippai Attena said. He jumped off the table and strode to the door.

"Didja think there was another kitchen on the second floor? It's almost lunchtime. I'll give you a bite of my lunch. Let's head back to the faculty room." Mr. Bear led us out into the hallway. He closed the door and tried to lock it. With all the keys jumbled up again, he had to rattle one key after another into the keyhole.

Humans didn't seem to be capable of much progress either.

Chapter 17

The Bear's Den

Mr. Bear came to school often during the summer holidays. Sometimes he was alone, and other times he was with other teachers. After finishing our lesson by the sandbox each morning, we went to peek in the faculty room. When Mr. Bear was there, he let us in. The faculty room was always nice and cool with the air conditioning on. When Mr. Bear wasn't there, we stole into classrooms through the small windows. Ippai Attena and I stayed in the school until evening when it was a little cooler outside.

Mr. Bear began to expect us, and tightly packed his huge lunch box so he had something to share. My favorite was wieners—it was the only time we got to eat meat these days.

When Mr. Bear didn't show up, we had to go somewhere else to find food. Sometimes we visited the witch, who was actually a kind old lady. We also went to see the young fishmonger. One thing we never did was scavenge garbage cans. Food quickly went bad in the summer heat and we didn't want to make ourselves sick. We were lucky because Ippai Attena knew a lot of people, and I knew some too.

Mr. Bear's real name was Uchida. I learned it when he was talking with another teacher. One evening, we tailed him to see where he lived. Mr. Bear walked from school to the shopping street. We followed at a distance, and saw him pop into one shop after another. By the time he was done, he had many bags of groceries in his thick arms.

"His house must be somewhere nearby," Ippai Attena explained to me. "If he commuted by train, he'd head towards the station, take a train and then shop when he got to his stop."

Mr. Uchida strode toward the river, not the station. He walked on and on until he got to a tobacco shop. A young woman came out.

"Hello, Sensei, coming straight home today?"

"Ha ha ha, I can't go out drinking every night."

I looked at Ippai Attena. "Do you think the bear usually drinks until late at night before coming home?" I asked. "Does he go to the river and drink water there?"

"Don't be stupid. Humans don't drink water in the river. It comes out of the tap. She's talking about sake."

"What? Sake? Is that some kind of fish he gets out of the river? Is it big like a salmon? In the new animal book, I saw a bear with a salmon in its mouth. D'you think Mr. Bear holds his salmon like that? He might really be a bear and not a human!"

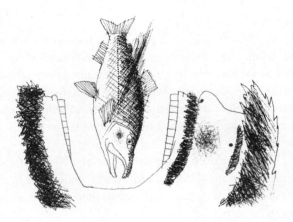

"Rudy, you're so ignorant. What man carries a fish in his mouth on his way home from school? You can't understand everything by just looking at illustrated books. He drinks sake, it's alcohol. Humans drink it to feel good. Or that's what I hear. A long time ago, my human forced me to drink some. Not very tasty and I felt awful afterwards."

While we were chatting, Mr. Bear, er, Uchida, went around the tobacco shop and then up the iron stairway outside a small apartment block. He disappeared behind one of the two doors on the second floor.

"Look, the bear lives here," said Ippai Attena.

"So this tobacco shop is the bear's den. Resi-DEN-ce of Mr. Uchida. Got it?" I joked. Ippai Attena rolled his eyes. I ignored him and went on.

"Then that young woman might be the bear's wife?"

"You really don't know anything," sighed my companion.

"Hey, you're the one who told me not to make fun of other cats for being uneducated!" I retorted.

"Sorry, sorry, just a slip. Listen, Rudy, no wife would say to her hubby, 'Hello, Sensei, coming straight home today?' Maybe he rents a room on the second floor." Just as Ippai Attena turned around to go, a window above the tobacco shop burst open.

"It's so hot in here . . . hey! You two, Boss and Blacky! I didn't expect to see you here."

Mr. Uchida was looking right out of the window. He had on only his shirt and shorts, and he looked more like a bear than ever—that might be why Ippai Attena and I never called him anything else after that.

We darted off as if we had been caught in some kind of mischief.

Chapter 18

Big Discovery

Every morning, I practiced learning kanji—about ten characters a day. They were more complicated than hiragana and katakana, but I was soon able to write them rather quickly. My paw got used to writing so many strokes without getting tired.

It was mid-August, the hottest time of year. Mr. Bear came to school every day. Every time he saw us, he said, "Lucky you! Cats have all the time in the world." But he didn't seem very busy. He would read books or sleep at his desk with his head on his arms. I remembered how, back home, Rie used to say the same thing. She was jealous because I didn't have to go to school or do homework.

"He's not coming here to work," whispered Ippai Attena one day after we had shared Mr. Bear's lunch with him. Licking my lips, I replied, "Think he comes to school to eat lunch, maybe?"

Ippai Attena frowned at me.

"Don't give me that look," I said. "All right, I'm an uneducated cat."

"You and your silly remarks—I've started thinking

maybe it's not just a lack of education. You learn letters quickly, so you must've got something between your ears, but sometimes I think you don't have even an ounce of sense."

Mr. Bear was watching TV. Recently, he was spending hours watching the annual national high school baseball tournament being held at a stadium called Koshien.

"He's got no air conditioning at home. That's my guess. He comes here to enjoy the cool, and the TV too," Ippai Attena muttered to himself. One baseball game had just finished, and the TV was showing some scenery to fill in the time and introduce the teams in the next game.

"Choshi faces the Pacific Ocean," the narration began. "This town has long been known for its fishing . . ."

The screen showed a vast expanse of water, like a big pond with no opposite shore in sight. That must be the Pacific Ocean, I realized. Sure enough, it was gigantic. The TV camera panned a port dotted with boats, and then fish wiggling on the floor of some fish market. I recognized them from an illustrated guide to fish: cutlassfish. Next, the screen changed to show students playing baseball on a school ground. I was getting drowsy—I had a full stomach, the air was cool, and my eyelids grew heavy.

"The opposing team is Gifu Commercial High School." Something about that name . . . I opened my drowsy eyes to glimpse at the screen.

"Gifu, the city famous for cormorant fishing in the Nagara River . . ." the announcer said.

"*Mee-YA-OW!*" I yelled, in surprise. My cry was so loud that Ippai Attena looked at me with a baffled expression. Mr. Bear also turned to see what was going on.

"Gosh, Blacky! What was that about?"

My eyes were riveted to the screen. The TV camera must have been on the top of a mountain, because it was showing a birds' eye view of a town with a river running through it. The announcer was saying something, but I'd stopped listening.

"Ippai *YA-OW* Attena!" My tongue was tied.

"What's the matter? What's got into you?" Seeing me staring at the TV, Ippai Attena turned to look back at the screen.

"That's it! My hometown!" I cried.

"You're kidding!" Ippai Attena was stunned.

"Yes, yes! I see the ropeway. Wow, the castle! No mistake. That's where I came from!"

"Shut up! Hush. I can't hear anything. Where's this town? Let me listen. Hmm, Gifu Commercial High School? I see now, Rudy. You lived in a town called Gifu," said Ippai Attena nodding his head, but I was bubbling over with excitement and just babbled. Ippai Attena moved closer to the TV and listened hard.

Once it was time for the baseball game to begin, the town disappeared from the screen. Ippai Attena came back to my side.

"Got it! Rudy, come along!" He shouted and ran to the door of the faculty room. Mr. Bear opened it for us. I ran after Ippai Attena, who entered the nearest classroom. Slipping through the desks, he sprinted to the bookshelf and looked it over from top to bottom.

"No, it's not here." Ippai Attena shook his head, and then darted out of the classroom. He didn't find whatever it was in the next classroom, either.

"What're you looking for?" I asked, running beside him.

"A map! Map of Japan."

"Map? There was one on the wall of the last classroom."

"Darn it! Why didn't you say so?" We ran back to find a map hanging on the wall. Ippai Attena jumped onto a desk by the roll-screen map and then leaped to strike the hook. The next moment, both the map and Ippai Attena were on the floor. Of course, Ippai Attena landed neatly on all fours.

"Rudy, hold down the map," he ordered, so I sat on one edge of it.

"Look. This is Tokyo. We're here," said Ippai Attena, pointing to a spot on the map. I already knew where Tokyo was because he had taught me.

"Well, the announcer said Chubu District. It must be somewhere around . . . hmm . . . Nagoya's here, Owariichinomiya's there. Oh, found it, right! This is Gifu."

The town Ippai Attena was pointing at was right in the center of the country.

Chapter 19

Expectation, Disappointment, and then Hope

That night, I couldn't get to sleep. I had found the name and location of the town I came from. I could go home! The next question was how to get there. During the day, Ippai Attena and I had studied the map and found the city of Nagoya in Aichi, a prefecture next to Gifu. In an illustrated book of vehicles, I had learned that the Hikari bullet train connected Tokyo and Nagoya, so I could take the Hikari to Nagoya, and it wouldn't be far to Gifu after that.

"I can take the bullet train home!" I said happily, but Ippai Attena looked worried.

"The train's OK, but I'm still not sure."

"Not sure of what?" I demanded. Ippai Attena, who had sprawled beside me, rose to his feet.

"Look, Rudy. I'm thrilled you can go home. I'll miss you, but we can talk about that later. There's something I have to tell you. I was thinking exactly the same thing. The bullet train leaves from Tokyo Station. But to get there from here, you have to change trains twice. See, we're on the eastern outskirts of Tokyo. Anyway the route is long and tricky. Even if you get to Tokyo Station, you'll have to get on the bullet train, go to Nagoya, then change trains again three, maybe four times . . . would you know which ones to take?"

"I can read simple kanji. I could memorize the stops in a few days. Trains have the destinations displayed above the front window, don't they?"

"Even then, Rudy, there are some more snags," Ippai Attena said. "You can't get a train ticket. Cats usually don't take trains. You could sneak in. But if the conductor catches you and throws you off, what then? Not all humans are nice."

"Yeah, I know," I admitted, but I still wasn't willing to give up. "What about a freight train?"

"I've already thought about that. You could hop on a freight train to Gifu, but it'll make lots of stops, and they don't announce station names. Roofless cars are dangerous. Container cars have heavy doors. You couldn't open them when you wanted to get off."

I was starting to feel blue, but I knew there had to be another way.

"If the train's no good, I could take a truck. That's how I got to Tokyo in the first place."

"Rudy, how will you know which truck is headed for Gifu? Remember the parking lot where you got off when you arrived here in Tokyo? Think of searching one truck after another there. You might find cargo destined for Gifu, then hide behind it, but there's no guarantee the driver wouldn't find you. Truck drivers usually load and unload at different spots. You just happened to be on a direct truck to Tokyo. Not all trucks go direct. Not all drivers are dimwits who don't notice a cat hiding in their cargo."

"What should I do then? I finally found the name of my hometown and I know where it is." I felt like crying. "If I can't get there, then I wish I'd never known!" I couldn't stop the tears falling.

"How dare you say such a thing!" said Ippai Attena. Now I'd made him mad again. "You know what they say, despair is the solace of fools." I had no idea what he was talking about and it just made me cry harder. "Now, now, don't rush to conclusions, half pint. We've got the name and location. Good ideas will come later." Ippai Attena changed his tone, maybe because he saw how upset I was.

That night, I went over and over our conversation, trying to figure a way out. When I finally drifted off, I had a dream about Rie.

The next morning, I woke up before sunrise. Beside me, Ippai Attena was still asleep, breathing evenly. I quietly walked out from under the verandah of the shrine. After a day of hopes and disappointments, I felt surprisingly calm.

Near our shrine was a building under construction. Work had started after I came to Tokyo, and a steel and concrete framework now stood on the site. I climbed up its stairway to the rooftop. The town was still asleep under the dim sky. I looked west in the direction of Gifu. It was so far, hundreds of kilometers away. I heard a bicycle bell on the street below. Must be the newspaper deliveryman. The town was about to awaken. Then suddenly, I saw a glow in the sky behind me. I turned around and was blinded by a brilliant red light.

Sunrise! A new day had begun.

The rising sun was painfully bright, but I stared straight at it. I saw the sun moving upward, slowly pushing up the dark of night. It was then that I realized I could be just like the sun in its path across the sky—if I was really determined, nothing could keep me from moving forward. I felt courage well up inside me. Once more, I looked back towards the west, and climbed down the stairs of the new building.

When I got back to the shrine, Ippai Attena was sitting on the stone steps under the *torii* shrine gate, waiting for me.

"Up early. Where've you been?"

"To the building construction site."

"For what?" Ippai Attena didn't usually pry like that.

"Nothing, I just went to see the sunrise. Well, it's gonna be hot again today. Let's get going."

"Huh? Where to?" Ippai Attena looked puzzled.

"Where to? School, of course. No kanji lessons today?"

"Oh, right! That's right. Yeah, sure, kanji lessons. What's wrong with me? Of course, let's go to study."

On the way to school, Ippai Attena said, "I woke up to find you gone. It shook me up, so I ran to the station, then to the parking lot where I first met you. Not a sign of you. Came back to the shrine and sat under the *torii*. I was so relieved when I saw your face."

"Did you think I'd gone back to Gifu?"

"Not really, I was just a little worried. That's all."

"Remember, I can't go by train or truck."

"Yeah, sure." Ippai Attena looked embarrassed.

"Then there's no way I can go home."

"But when I didn't see you in the parking lot, I wondered if you'd decided to walk. Although it seemed very unlikely."

"Listen, Ippai Attena. I may walk home if I can't find any other way. Gifu and Tokyo are connected by land. But I'll never leave you without saying goodbye." I pretended to be offended that he'd think otherwise.

"Ha ha ha, don't get so mad, kid. Yeah, right. I wasn't myself. You wouldn't leave without letting me know." Ippai Attena had been anxious about me because I had gone through a lot yesterday. I pretended to be offended, but actually I was pleased.

If worst came to worst, I'd walk home. I was resolved. But not now. I still had things to do in Tokyo. Rie and the girl at the ropeway station must be worried about me, but that couldn't be helped. I'd learn a little more. At least, I'd learn to read and write kanji as well as the children at school. Then I'd go home. It might take another year, but if I quit now, all my efforts would be wasted. I could walk home if I really had to. As long as I believed in myself. All of a sudden, I could feel energy surging through every part of my body.

Afterwards, I studied kanji harder than ever in my sandbox classroom. When summer vacation was over, we moved to the sandbox in the park next to the shrine.

Chapter 20

What the Typhoon Brought

Tokyo was hit twice by typhoons during the second half of September. The first one wasn't so bad, but the second one was terrible. The wind raged and drove the rain against the roof and walls of the shrine. The shrine was built on grounds higher than the streets, so our home under the floor didn't get very wet. But the roads around the shrine were all flooded and looked like a river.

When night fell, the typhoon got even stronger. We heard blustery winds screaming in the gingko trees. Objects blown by the wind crashed against the roof. Roof tiles came loose and dropped right in front of our noses, shattering into pieces.

"Good grief, a monster of a typhoon! Maybe we should have fled to safety earlier. This place may not hold." I knew Ippai Attena was only trying to scare me, but I was getting nervous.

"It's too late to go anywhere. All the roads are flooded. What should we do?"

"Don't worry, kid. When push comes to shove, we can swim. You can swim, right?" His question alarmed me. Could I swim? No, not a single stroke. I'd never been in deep water, or even in a puddle in the sidewalk.

"To tell the truth, no." I confessed.

"Seriously? Can't swim? Gee, that's bad."

I had never dreamed I'd be in such a fix. Now I wished he would have taught me how. The elementary school had a pool after all. What good was kanji in a situation like this?

"So, Ippai Attena," I sighed, "I imagine you're a great swimmer."

Ippai Attena rolled his eyes at me.

"Me? Swim? Don't be silly. Just thought I might ask you to swim out and bring me some food. But since you can't, we'll have to stay hungry till tomorrow morning. Bad luck."

What? He couldn't swim, but he didn't mind asking me to go out in a storm? I looked at him with my mouth open.

"Hey, don't look at me like that! I was just kidding." Ippai Attena laughed. Now that he mentioned it, though, I was getting hungry too. We'd seen a bucket and scrap lumber flying about, but nothing good like a slice of tuna. I wished a fish store would be blown into the sky and fall right into the shrine—who knew? It might happen. I stuck my head outside to check, just in case.

Whap! Something sopping wet hit my face and stuck there. Blindly waving my paws, I struggled to peel it off, but it was held fast by the howling wind. I didn't know what had happened. Then it covered my entire head, and finally the soppy thing started to wrap around my body. It felt like a wet newspaper. With much difficulty, I managed to wriggle back into our space beneath the veranda.

"Hey! He-elp! S-something on m-my f-face . . . He-e-lp!"

"What? Ha ha ha! Look at yourself! Stop squirming, or that thing'll never come off. Hey, don't move. I'll peel it off for you. Stay still!" I was suffocating under the wet paper covering my mouth and nose, so I couldn't help myself from kicking out.

And then suddenly I was able to breathe freely. Ippai Attena had used his claws to tear a hole in the wet paper, and when I stuck my face through it, Ippai Attena cracked up.

"Hilarious! Never seen a cat wearing a poncho! You might as well take a walk in the rain."

I stuck out my feet to make the hole bigger and squirmed out of the paper.

"What's this? A huge piece of paper. Ouch! Pushpins!"

"Must be a poster blown off the wall somewhere. Why don't you wear it and parade around town? Its owner may give you a fish or something in appreciation for the free advertising. Keep your poncho till tomorrow, I say."

"Hey, it's mean to laugh at people's misfortunes!" I

was getting angry.

"Jeez, I helped you, and you're crabby. Also what about 'people's misfortunes,' eh? When did you become people? Never knew you belonged to the human race—no inkling until today. Life is full of surprises."

Ippai Attena must have been bored, stuck under the shrine in this typhoon. I was the only entertainment available, and he was having fun pulling my leg. But I was getting irritated. Holding the edge of the poster in my mouth, I pressed the other end with my paw and tore it into two. I pushed the torn pieces outside, and the wind swept them away.

The typhoon moved on during the night, and morning brought a clear blue sky.

"Hey, Rudy, on a day like this, there's a good chance we can get a feast. Let's go grab it before the others do!" Ippai Attena was already outside. I yawned and rose to my feet.

"What's the feast?"

"Big carp. Some houses have ponds in them that must have flooded during the storm. Goldfish and carp were probably escaping from them all night. Now that the flood water is down, the fish are probably flopping around up and down the road."

"Hot dog! Which way?"

"We'll go look for them. Come out, quick. Weather's great too. Get a move on!"

Ippai Attena's voice became fainter as he set off. He might actually go without me, and I didn't want to miss a chance for fresh fish. I hurried out, but he had already disappeared.

"Hey, where are you?" I yelled as I walked towards the *torii*. Then I caught sight of Ippai Attena under the gingko tree. He had his back to me, but I could see he was looking up at something.

"Wait a sec! I'm coming." I started running.

"Look!" he said, without taking his eyes off of whatever was so interesting. "You may be able to go home earlier than we thought."

I followed his gaze and saw something whitish hanging on a low branch of the gingko tree. What the heck! It was half of that nasty poster.

"Rudy, read it," urged Ippai Attena.

"Ooh!" I cried when I started reading, and the next moment, I was shouting. I saw the kanji for Gifu (岐阜)!

Of course, I couldn't read all the characters on the poster. I understood "shopping street" (商店街), and then there was another word that Ippai Attena told me meant "autumn colors" (紅葉). I also saw the word "bus" (バス) next to two kanji that Ippai Attena told me meant "trip" (旅行). The poster was advertising a bus trip to Gifu to see the autumn colors, and it must be sponsored by the stores in a shopping street!

"Rudy, this shopping-street poster is the same one

that got stuck to your face yesterday. I'm sure I saw that same picture of a bus on it. It was dark so I didn't get a good look, but I'm sure that's it. I should have read the print last night. You tore it in half, so the bottom part with the details is missing. We've got to find it!"

We searched the shrine for the rest of the poster. We'd been lucky to find the upper half, but the lower part must have swirled away somewhere.

"Ippai Attena, it's gone. Yesterday's storm was crazy," I said, but then I got an idea. "Do you think it's a poster from our local shopping street?"

"I was wondering the same thing. If it is, we'll probably see another one just like it!"

In an instant, we darted off. We searched all the nooks and crannies of shops, walls, and fences on the shopping street in our neighborhood, but found none. We went back and forth, over and over, in case we'd missed it.

"Ippai Attena, if the poster is not from this street, it must be from another one."

"Maybe so, but it can't be very far. If the wind had carried the poster over a distance, it wouldn't have got here in one piece." We then went to all the shopping streets in town—two in the neighborhood and one on the other side of the train tracks, but again found nothing.

We walked all day and came back to our shopping street, starving. When we passed the fish shop, our fishmonger called out to us.

"Hey, you two look miserable. What happened?" We didn't have the energy to reply.

"Like dying ducks in a thunderstorm. Hungry, eh? Hmm, nothing much to give you today, but here you are. Share this fish!" The fishmonger took the single fish left in the showcase, cut it in two, and threw the halves to us.

"One left. I was going to eat it for dinner, but that's OK." Without even the time to be polite and thank him, we gobbled it up. Ippai Attena ate the head, and I got the tail.

"Wow, scarfing it down. Don't gorge, or you'll choke on a bone. But you two get on great, don't you? Even for us humans, it's hard to find really good friends."

What was he so impressed with? The young man squatted to watch us eat. When we finished, we purred a thank you and left.

"I should have known we'd never have any good ideas on an empty stomach. That's for sure. Anyway, let's not waste time continuing the search," said Ippai Attena. "While eating the fish, it came to me. That poster is from a shopping street. What about our Butchy? I wonder if he knows about shopping street events." Ippai Attena was right! Butchy lived in the hardware store. He might know something. We went around to the back of his shop.

"Hey, Butchy, are you there?" Ippai Attena shouted up toward the second floor window.

"Not so loud, Ippai Attena. Butchy is scared of you. Here, let me do it." I called out for him.

"What do you want? I'm here." We heard Butchy's voice. He was standing right behind us. Turning around, Ippai Attena bawled at him.

"Whaddaya mean creeping up on us from behind!"

Butchy just stood there, too frightened to speak.

"Ippai Attena, don't yell at him."

"Back off, Rudy! I'll get a confession out of him. Now, spit it out. Tell Stripes everything you know. Cover up anything, and you'll pay for it."

Butchy took a shaky step backward.

"You punk! Think you can get away from me?" Ippai Attena looked about to leap onto the frightened cat. The moment he lowered his body to gather momentum, I barred his way.

"Calm down, Ippai Attena! You won't find out anything by threatening him! How can he confess if he doesn't know what you're talking about?" Butchy cowered behind us. "Look, he's frightened. Why can't you be gentler? You're always so nice to me," I reasoned.

"He's only nice to abandoned cats and strays. He was abandoned himself, so he sympathizes with cats like you," Butchy managed to whisper into my ear. Ippai Attena heard him and snarled.

"Say that again, squirt!"

Spitting this out, he pounced towards Butchy, but I

was a split second faster. Ippai Attena's body hit me hard, and I was hurled into the air. I almost fell right into the ditch. Ippai Attena rushed toward me in a panic.

"Rudy, you . . . you all right?"

Butchy saw his chance and tried to sneak away, but Ippai Attena shouted after him.

"Butchy, run now and you'll have to keep running for the rest of your miserable life!"

Butchy froze.

"Stop, Ippai Attena! Please. Let me talk to him," I said, as I moved toward the tabby.

"Hey, I'm sorry, Butchy. Ippai Attena's a little edgy after the typhoon last night. Forgive him, will you?"

Butchy just sobbed. "I don't know what he wants to hear! What'm I supposed to confess?"

"I apologize. We have our reasons."

"I don't know about your reasons. They've got nothing t'do with me!"

Ippai Attena butted in.

"Nothin' to do with you? That's not the issue here. You've got information we need and you better not hold any back!"

"I said, leave us alone for a minute! Butchy can't talk if you're around." I was firm this time.

"All right, all right. I'll take a walk around the neighborhood," Ippai Attena grumbled and sauntered off toward the main street. He looked back a few times before he finally turned the corner and disappeared.

"OK, he's gone now," I reassured Butchy. "Sorry about that. Now I wanna ask you something. But before that, let me tell you my story. Otherwise, you won't understand what we're doing." I then told Butchy that I had discovered I was from Gifu and that I wanted to get back there.

When I was done, Butchy nodded, but still looked dubious. "Now I understand. But what does it have to do with me?"

"We found a poster for a bus tour sponsored by a local merchants' association, and the destination is Gifu. Of course, the poster may not be from your street. We just don't know. We wanted to know if you'd seen it or knew something about it, Butchy. Since you're the hardware store cat, you know that sort of thing."

Butchy tilted his head. He thought for a few moments. "Tour? By bus? Hmmm . . . I wonder if . . ."

"Do you know something?" I was excited.

"I don't know if this one goes to Gifu, but I've heard about a bus trip. The other day, my owner was talking with a customer about some trip. You said something about a poster? A poster is a big piece of paper you put up as an advertisement, right? There's no such poster in my store. And if we don't have it, none of the other stores will either. Everyone usually puts them up at the same time. Now, where did you see this one?"

"It was blown to our place by the typhoon yesterday," I replied.

"Merchants' associations love this kind of bus trip, but I haven't seen or heard about this one. That means yours belongs somewhere else. The one thing I'm sure of," he concluded confidently, "is that the poster had to come from somewhere or it never would have blown to your place."

I couldn't ignore his logic. If it wasn't from here it must have come from somewhere else. Probably farther away. And we knew for a fact that somewhere, some place, a bus trip to Gifu was being planned. It was too early to give up hope.

"Well, then. Butchy, let me know if you happen to see the poster."

"Sure, I'll let you know. But tell Stripes to lay off me. There's no telling what he'll do when he goes off like that." I promised him I would ask Ippai Attena to be nicer and less of a bully.

"One more thing," said Butchy, as I was about to leave. "Tell Stripes I shouldn't have made that comment about him being abandoned. I know it hurt his feelings. I'm sorry about that. Tell him, will you? Bye!"

I walked in the direction Ippai Attena had gone. When I turned the corner, I found him sitting and waiting for me.

"Hey, find out anything?" Ippai Attena looked

impatient. I told him everything I had heard from Butchy. Of course, I asked him not to rough up our pal again. I also told him that Butchy apologized to him.

"I see. So we know that if a poster wasn't posted on the wall, it wouldn't be blown away. But it's not from this street. Hmm, back to square one. But wait! We assumed the poster had been put up at some store, but it may have been put away somewhere, in a warehouse or storage. Then something happened and it just flew away. That would be a totally different story. Look, Rudy, have you seen any house with the roof torn away by the wind?"

No, I hadn't, but I remembered the pushpins. They must have been keeping the poster on a wall. Ippai Attena knew that too, but said the poster might have been stored somewhere. He obviously didn't want to see me disappointed.

We hadn't quite given up, and still clung to a thread of hope. In the meantime, we went back to our den under the shrine. "Despair is the solace of fools," you know.

Chapter 21

Ippai Attena's Hard-luck Story

Two days, three days, and more days passed. We went to the school sandbox early every morning to practice reading and writing. After my lesson, we went to look for food or take a walk. In other words, Ippai Attena and I were leading life as usual. There was no word from Butchy. We walked through the shopping street every day, but saw no posters in any of the shops.

One morning in the sandbox, I asked Ippai Attena a question.

"Look, Ippai Attena. You're really rough on other cats. The other day, you jumped on Butchy, who had done nothing wrong. But you're so nice to me. Is it because I'm a stray? Because you feel sorry for me? Tell me why you're so rough on the other cats?"

"I told you before. If I were nice to the others, I wouldn't survive—couldn't get any food."

"But I don't get it. With Butchy, we weren't fighting for food." I persisted, but Ippai Attena just sniffed and turned away. There was no way I could press him further, so I started practicing kanji again. Then, Ippai Attena murmured something, still looking the other way.

"I hate them all, cats and dogs who have nice homes."

"But you were a house cat before, weren't you?" I said, trying to sound casual.

"Yeah, I was a house cat. But I wasn't as selfish as those cats."

"Those cats? You mean Butchy?" I asked bluntly, careful to keep my eyes on the character I was writing and not look my friend straight in the eye.

"Butchy? No, he's not so bad."

I finally raised my head and asked, "Then who are those cats?"

Ippai Attena was silent, looking into the distance. Then he said in a low voice,

"House cats I used to run around with a long time ago. And Devil."

I was itching to find out more, but I knew my eagerness would only put him off. So I simply said, "Is that so?"

"My human fed me what he ate. Pretty good food—fried shrimp, hamburger, steak, and often sukiyaki. I used to eat grade A beef dipped in raw egg. My human would break an egg in my plate and dip slices of beef in it. In summer time, we had dinner on the porch, enjoying the cool of the night. When neighbor cats dropped into our garden, my human threw them some meat. I let him because I had enough to eat. When I was full, I even let the others eat from my plate. Then when I met them on the street, they bowed and scraped. 'Hello, Mr. Tiger. Taking a walk? Do drop by at my house for a visit.'

"But then my human left the house and abandoned me. There was no one to feed me. I went around the neighborhood to see those pet cats, hoping they'd share food. Too naïve, I guess," Ippai Attena continued without looking at me. "What do you think happened? Once I became a stray, they changed their attitudes completely. They'd say their owners didn't want them hanging out with strays, or there was only enough food for one cat. Some even said, 'I was friends with your owner, not you.' That was when I realized I had only myself to rely on.

"Since then, I hate even the sight of a cat with a home. Then there's Devil the bulldog. I'll never forgive him as long as I live. His house was right next to ours, with a hedge in between. Now my owner's house is torn down and it's a vacant lot. The hedge was replaced with a concrete wall. Devil runs around loose on the other side. In the old days, he used to come to the hedge and whimper for attention. He cajoled my owner into giving him steak and other goodies. But now that I'm a stray, Devil howls at me whenever I pass his garden. When he has some leftovers and I try to steal them from his plate, he just goes crazy, running after me with his bloodshot eyes. If he were a cat, I wouldn't leave him alone. But he's such an enormous dog, I can't do anything."

What a beast of a dog! It's dogs like him that make humans despise cats and dogs.

"If it were only me, I'd try my best to put up with the big lug. It's not why I hate him so much."

"You mean there's something even worse?" I blurted out, no longer able to stay quiet.

"D'you know what that dog said about my human, who had treated him so nicely? He said, 'Your owner escaped in the middle of night to avoid paying back money he borrowed,' and 'you say your owner went to North America, but who knows if that's true? Maybe North America is just another word for prison.' Devil even said, 'The meat he gave me was rotten. I forced the stuff down, but puked it up later.'" Ippai Attena's eyes smoldered with hatred. But then a moment later he gave a lonely-looking smile.

"You see, I've had my share of hardship." Then he continued in a brighter tone of voice. "Yeah, you're a stray, like me. At first I felt sorry for you and took care of you. But I've come to like you. I mean, you're cheerful, you don't push others out of the way." Ippai Attena continued, "I feel like a better cat when I'm with you." He looked a little embarrassed, and as I was trying to figure out how to respond, just at that moment, we heard someone calling.

"Ahoy! Rudy! Rudolf!"

It was Butchy.

Chapter 22

Good News

Butchy was racing toward us at full speed. Just looking at him, I knew that the poster was up in his store.

"Hey, Rudolf," he cried out, panting. "P-p-poster! It's up! Hanging everywhere in the shop street!"

Ippai Attena drew closer to him.

"What, Butchy? Say it again."

Butchy hunched his shoulders and cowered away, afraid of what my pal might do.

"I said the poster's up."

"OK, that's my boy, Butchy! Rudy, let's go see it!" Ippai Attena took off like a shot. I stayed long enough to say, "Thanks, Butchy!" and sprinted after him. To my surprise, Ippai Attena suddenly came to a stop, turned around, and stood still for a moment. Then he took a few steps back and called out to Butchy.

"Sorry for the other day. Let's be friends . . . if you want. You're not bad for a house cat." Then he ran off again. Of course, I rushed after him. As we went, we heard Butchy's voice from behind us.

"Stripes, whaddaya mean 'if you want'? I've always wanted to be friends with you! You taught Rudolf how to read and write. Wouldja teach me how to fight? Wouldja?"

Ippai Attena and I grinned at each other and kept on running.

By now it was time for kids to be on their way to school. There were a few in our way as we were about to zip out of the main gate, but even the older boys made way for us as we charged towards them.

"What's got into them?" one said.

"Are they racing?" said another.

"D'ya think cats race?" said a third boy.

We heard someone yell, "Watch where you're going!" Then there was the screech of a bicycle braking, and the sound of a crash. A cyclist must have lost his balance trying to avoid us. But nothing stopped us. We ran and ran and ran.

Finally, we turned a corner and were in the shopping street. The first shop we saw was the pharmacy. And there on its glazed glass door was the poster! Yippee!

"So it was from this shopping street after all!" I shouted.

"Shut up and read," said Ippai Attena, gazing at the poster. "It says November 2. That's one month from now. Rudy, kid, you can go home!" Ippai Attena was as happy as if he himself were going. I was speechless with joy.

"A chartered bus. That means you don't need to transfer. Sneak in, and you can go directly to Gifu or

Inuyama. Gifu must be the first stop. Rudy, you said you used to go on a ropeway. It must be one of the spots they'll visit. When you get there, watch for a chance to get off the bus. Then you'll know where to go. Ha ha ha, we've done it, Rudy. Hey, now look at your face."

Ippai Attena was in high spirits. I was so happy I wanted to cry. If some human had been watching us, they'd have wondered what the two cats were doing together—one wailing loudly and the other sniffling away tears.

"Only one month till your departure. Maybe I'll go with you. After I leave you in Gifu, I'll just get back on the bus and take it back to Tokyo. I could hide under a seat or slip into the baggage compartment. While shopping-street customers are enjoying the castle and autumn leaves, I'll go visit your Rie. Ha, ha, ha! Shall we take Butchy too? I hate to think of coming back home alone, but he'll probably say no. Such a coward! Butchy'd be scared of taking even a step outside this town." Ippai Attena was getting carried away. By this time, Butchy had finally caught up with us, and he had heard the last bit of our conversation.

"No bus trip for me. I hate buses. The other day, my human put me in the van. I got carsick and threw up. You go right ahead, buddies," said Butchy. But he looked pleased. "I'll miss you, Rudy. But when you're gone, there'll be no kanji lessons, so Stripes here can teach me fighting techniques. No more napping for me! The school sandbox will turn into my dojo. I wish you were leaving sooner!" I could tell he didn't really mean it. It was just his way of being happy for me.

We confirmed the day, time, and location of the bus departure: November 2, 6:00 a.m., south end of the shopping street. The one thing I knew for sure was that I'd be there. I'd probably sit there all night waiting. And then I'd sneak on the bus the instant it pulled up. By evening, I'd be back with Rie, cuddled up in her arms again.

We three cats spent the whole morning strolling up and down the shopping street and howling. Only when we got to the hardware shop did we calm down and jog quietly past. We didn't want Butchy's owner to think his cat was hanging out with a bad crowd of strays. Of course, we made up for this by kicking up a din in front of the fish shop.

Chapter 23

Preparing for Departure

The time of my departure drew closer. I studied hard with Ippai Attena every morning, trying to learn as many kanji as possible before leaving. When I read newspapers I found littering the street, I couldn't understand many characters, but when Ippai Attena was with me, I could ask him how to read them. When I go back to Gifu, there won't be anyone to teach me, I thought. I may forget the kanji I've learned. When I mentioned this to Ippai Attena, he said, "No need to worry. There's something to help you out with that. Let's sneak into a classroom tomorrow morning, and I'll teach you how to use it. Not a problem!"

Early next morning, we stole into a classroom. Ippai Attena said it was one where the sixth graders—the oldest kids—studied. Ippai Attena stood in front of the bookshelf, and then jumped to pull out a thick book with a yellow cover on the top shelf. It moved a little on the first jump, and on the next one, thumped onto the floor. The cover had four kanji characters 漢和辞典 on it. I knew only the second one.

"Something, *wa* (和), something, something. What's

this about?" I asked.

"With this book, you no longer need to say 'something, something.' It's a dictionary of kanji characters." Ippai Attena replied.

"Dictionary of kanji?"

"That's right. This book tells you how to read each kanji character."

Indeed it was for looking up both the meaning and reading of kanji. Ippai Attena taught me how to use it—it took a whole hour.

"Gee, this is great! I wonder if Rie has one."

"You'll find a dictionary or two at any house. Now let's have a look at another book." Ippai Attena jumped to take down the next book on the shelf. The cover read 国語辞典, Japanese Dictionary.

"This one's for checking up the meaning of Japanese words. They are arranged in the order of the syllabary, *aiueo*—just like I taught you." Ippai Attena then showed me the definition for a dictionary: *a book that puts words in a specific order and describes the meaning of each*.

"Wow, this one's useful as well. I can use it for both words and kanji. Does every house have this dictionary too?"

Ippai Attena nodded. "Sure! There's also something called an encyclopedia. They don't have a set here, but it'll help you get every conceivable kind of information from around the world. It's actually a series of many books. Lots of illustrations, too. Your owner may have one. But each book is heavy and comes in a case. Cats can't handle them easily," Ippai Attena explained, as if he owned the place.

With these dictionaries, I could study by myself. I was relieved.

"But, Rudy, be careful," said Ippai Attena, as if reading my mind. "If you get to thinking you can study any time, you may end up doing nothing. Thinking it's now or never is probably safer. Studying by yourself—it's easier said than done. As for me, I learned how to read and write because my owner really pushed me."

There were so many errands to do before my departure. I had to say goodbye to many people who were kind to me. The witch, the ladies at the school kitchen, the young fishmonger, our friend the police officer.

We understand human language, but humans don't understand cats. So when I went to say goodbye, they must have thought I was just meowing. But it was OK. It was important to me to do it properly. When I was gone, those people would realize I'd been saying goodbye.

The last person I visited was Mr. Bear. It was evening and his window on the second floor of the tobacco shop was brightly lit. We meowed up toward the window. It rattled open, and Mr. Bear put his face out. I could see he had something in his hand.

"There you are, Boss and Blacky! I haven't seen you lately and was worried maybe you'd been blown away by the typhoon. I'm coming. Hold on a sec," he said and closed the window.

"Ippai Attena, he was holding something strange in his hand."

"A paintbrush, I guess."

"Paintbrush?"

"Yeah, a tool humans use for writing and drawing."

While we were chatting, Mr. Bear came down and said, "Nice timing. I'm just about done. Now I can play with cats or something."

"Cats or something" again, I thought. Can't he refer to us without saying "something"?

"My mom sent me dried fish. Do you want some?" We responded with a loud meow.

"Let's see. Can I carry you both? Don't wiggle. I'm not supposed to bring animals into my room." So saying, Mr. Bear took us up in his arms. His hands had spots of red, green, and many other colors. What was he doing up there?

When we got in, he dropped us onto the tatami mats. His room was a complete mess. A lot of small tubes with labels in different colors were scattered everywhere. Sticks with bristles at the tip—the things Ippai Attena called "paintbrushes"—were also lying on the tatami. By the wall stood a wooden frame that contained a half-finished painting. Mr. Bear was a painter. He was a teacher at school, a painter at home.

Mr. Bear closed the door with a bang. It was so loud that we both looked back at it in surprise. Lo and behold, on the back of the door was the poster from the shopping street! Ippai Attena and I exchanged glances. Noticing that both of us were staring at the poster, Mr. Bear said, "I painted that. Good, isn't it? It's a print. The original had better color. I put it up there. But on the night of the typhoon, the wind forced the door open and snatched my original painting away. Too bad."

Ippai Attena and I exchanged glances again—the wind had carried his painting to us that night! Mr. Bear was still talking.

"Have you seen this poster in the shopping street? They asked me to paint it—that's how good I am!"

That night, we stayed at Mr. Bear's room till late. He was doing another painting. We ate the dried fish he gave us and watched him work.

"Sit for me one of these days. I'll draw you two together."

I appreciated the thought, but I was pretty sure that wouldn't happen. I was going home soon.

Chapter 24

Foul Play

Only two more days to go! The day after tomorrow, I would be home by evening. Just the thought of it made me smile. When I was practicing kanji in the school sandbox in the morning, I found myself writing 帰る (go home) over and over. The last couple of days, Butchy had also come along with us. He seemed hardly able to wait for his turn to learn from Ippai Attena. He sat right beside us and interrupted me now and then.

"Hey, little Rudy, you're going home the day after tomorrow. It'll be a long trip, so why don't you rest up a little? Stripes, let's practice fighting!"

"No rush, Butchy. After I get back from Gifu, I'll have plenty of time for your training. For now, don't distract Rudolf, or I won't teach you anything. And stop saying 'fighting.' 'The art of self-defense' sounds much more educated."

Ippai Attena seemed rather pleased about the idea of teaching Butchy the so-called art of self-defense. I didn't know how it was any different from fighting, so I asked Ippai Attena.

"You use the same techniques in a fight and for self-defense. But, hmm, how can I explain it?" he began. "The spirit is different. Self-defense is for protecting yourself. You've got to understand the spirit. You listening too, Butchy?"

"Sure! I get it," replied Butchy. But I wondered if he really did.

That night, I went to the south end of the shopping street where the bus was to depart. I knew it so well that I didn't need to check, but I was too excited to sleep and there was no one back at the shrine. Butchy had come to pick up Ippai Attena and the two had gone off somewhere. That morning they had been talking in a whisper, so I knew they were up to something. "We're looking for a place for our self-defense practice," Ippai Attena had told me. "You stay here."

There was nothing unusual happening at the south end of the shopping street, so I came right back. Ippai Attena wasn't home yet. I got bored and started thinking of climbing up on the shrine roof. We were well into autumn, so the night was chilly.

While I debated whether I should risk catching a cold so near to my departure, I saw a cat darting toward me from the other side of the *torii*. I couldn't tell for sure in the dark, but it looked like Butchy. I had a bad feeling.

"Oh, Rudy! Something awful has happened!" It was definitely Butchy. He was shouting and running at the same time.

"What? What're you talking about?" I shouted back at him while he was still at a distance.

"Stripes got beat up," gasped Butchy as he came closer.

Beat up? I felt the blood draining from my face.

"Is Ippai Attena hurt? Who did it? What happened?" I asked. Butchy was with me now, but he was out of breath and too agitated to respond right away. Finally he managed to get out the story.

"It was Devil! That beast played a dirty trick on Stripes."

"Devil? Did they fight?"

"Th-that's right."

"What's happened to Ippai Attena? Where is he?"

"In the lot next to Devil's house. He's bleeding badly; he can't walk. R-Rudy, w-what shall we d-d-do?"

"Bleeding? Can't walk? Darn it! Why didn't you say so first!" I was already off running.

The vacant lot next to Devil's house was where Ippai Attena's house used to be. I jumped over hedges and scurried down the thin trails of concrete block walls between houses. I was usually careful when crossing the street, but I just zipped across roads without looking right and left for cars. Finally I saw the vacant lot. I yelled, still running, "Ippai Attena, Ippai Attena! Where are you?"

I didn't see him at first.

"Ippai Attena, Ippai Attena! Where are you, IPPAI ATTENA?" My cry echoed in the night sky.

Woof! Woof! In the garden next to the lot, Devil was barking triumphantly.

You Devil! What did you do to Ippai Attena? For a moment, I was ready to jump up onto the wall of his garden. But no! I needed to rescue my friend.

"Ippai Attena! It's me, Rudolf! Where are you? Answer me!"

There was no answer, and I got more and more anxious. Even if he was hurt, he should be able to at least say something. What if . . . ? Then, I saw Butchy by the wall. He had finally caught up with me.

"Rudy, not there! This way. Here! Come here!"

I bolted to the spot where Butchy was standing and in the dim moonlight saw Ippai Attena's striped body lying face-down at the foot of the wall in a clump of grass.

"Are you all right, Ippai Attena?" I called out to him, but he didn't reply, not even a twitch. As I pressed my face against the back of his neck, I felt something slimy on my nose. Blood! He was bleeding from his shoulder. I put my face against Ippai Attena's back.

He was breathing faintly. He was alive! What could I do? Devil was on the other side of the wall, unable to attack us. But I couldn't carry Ippai Attena back to the shrine. He was much too big. But if I left him here, he'd certainly die.

"What are we gonna do?" asked Butchy.

I didn't have a clue . . . there was nothing we could do . . . but then an idea flashed into my mind.

"Butchy, stay here and guard Ippai Attena. Devil can't jump over the wall. But there might be another stray dog around who could hurt him. I'll be right back!"

"Where're you going, Rudy?" wailed Butchy, but I couldn't stay to answer. The witch's house was nearby. I raced there at full speed.

She wasn't home. At least, there were no lights on. I meowed at her wooden door with all my might, but there wasn't a sound in return. I scratched the door hard, but still nothing. Had she already gone to bed? I didn't have time to stop and think about it. If the witch wasn't home, my next stop would be Mr. Bear.

I crossed the gardens of many houses and leaped over drum cans, almost tumbling as I landed. I kept running, but could feel my pace slackening. I was starting to feel out of breath and began to pant. My heart was pounding so hard I thought it would burst. Finally I was in the neighborhood.

As soon as I turned the next corner, I'd see the tobacco shop. *Please let Mr. Bear be home!* I prayed. As far as I knew, there were gods living in our shrine, but it was the first time I'd ever called out to them for help.

My prayer was answered! The lights were on in Mr.

Bear's apartment. He was at home. I ran to the spot directly beneath his window and yowled at the top of my lungs.

Meow! Meow-meow, Mee-YOW! I saw his silhouette in the window, and then it rattled open.

"What? What's the noise?" Mr. Bear looked down, his eyes searching for me.

Mee-YOW! It's me, Blacky. MEE-YOW! Mr. Bear seemed unable to make me out in the dark. It was the first time I ever regretted being a black cat. I moved close to a big vending machine, which shed light on the ground.

"Oh, it's you, Blacky. What's the matter with you, wailing like that?"

Mee-YOW! I didn't stop.

"What? Now that's weird," said Mr. Bear, "he's not his usual self. All right, I'm coming down."

Thank goodness he had realized something was wrong. He stomped down the stairs. I copied what Ippai Attena had done before in the school hallway when he tried to lead the man to the library. When he came near me, I took several steps away from him. Again he moved toward me, and again I moved away.

"Ah, trying to take me somewhere. Not the library again, I hope. Cats have no business there," he mumbled. I started running, making sure Mr. Bear was following me. This time, I had to take the regular roads. I couldn't go under hedges or cross people's gardens. My companion—even though he looked like a bear—wouldn't be able to follow. I turned around many, many times to see if he was with me, and he did his best to keep up. We were getting close to the vacant lot. I could see Butchy standing on the street in front of it. He must have heard me coming.

"Hey, Rudy. It's been ages. Where were you?" Seeing a man running behind me, Butchy jumped onto the wall. "What the heck? Who's that big guy? Ah, whoa! It's the school teacher."

I had no time to explain things to Butchy. I went over and stood by Ippai Attena's limp body and wailed.

MEE-YOOW!

Mr. Bear tramped into the lot, saying "What is it, Blacky? Wait, what've you got there?" He stooped down, and as soon as he saw the sprawling body at my side, he yelled, "It's Boss! W-what happened?" He stooped over Ippai Attena and put a hand on his breast.

"OK, he's alive. Bleeding badly, but alive." Mr. Bear carefully picked up Ippai Attena and moved under the streetlamp.

"This is really bad. Must be a dog, bitten by a dog. Hmm. I should take him to an expert. I can't dress a wound like this . . . Wait, I know!"

With that he darted off. This time, it was me who was running after Mr. Bear. Butchy came along too. Mr.

Bear was heading towards the station—with two cats on his trail.

"Clear the way! Clear the way!" he called out to passers-by as he ran. At the front of the station, Mr. Bear turned right and ran along the railway. Up the road, I saw a lit-up signboard. It said Family Pet Clinic, and had an illustration of cats and dogs. Running beside me, Butchy said, "He's going to take Stripes to a vet!"

The clinic was still open, and Mr. Bear went inside with Ippai Attena in his arms. Butchy and I rushed to the front door, but it slammed in our face. We howled outside, hoping someone would open it. Finally, Mr. Bear stuck his face out and shouted, "Hush! Don't distract the vet, or he won't be able to save Boss." We had no choice but to wait patiently in front of the clinic.

"Hey, Butchy, what happened? How did he get hurt?" I asked when it looked like we were going to be there for a while.

"Well, you're leaving the day after tomorrow. So Stripes said, 'Let's give Rudolf a feast tonight.'"

"A feast for me? But why did he have to get hurt for that?"

"You didn't have any meat lately, right? And cream stew hasn't been on the menu since summer vacation ended. Stripes asked me where he might be able to get some meat. Unfortunately, my owner never has any around. Then I remembered Devil sometimes gets some nice beef. I said, 'How about Devil's house? He eats meat.' Come to think of it, I shouldn't have said that. It was this morning. We lied to you about going to look for a training ground. Stripes and I actually went to see Devil. We didn't go there to steal. Stripes was going to ask the dog to spare some leftovers for you, Rudolf. That was his plan."

Butchy gave a sigh. I didn't say anything, so he continued his story with his eyes downcast.

"After what's happened to him, this may sound like an excuse, but I did tell him not to go. Stripes hates Devil. Why should he have to beg that nasty dog to give him a bit of meat?" Butchy looked at me as if he wanted me to agree with him.

"I told him to give up on his idea but Stripes insisted. 'It's a farewell for Rudolf. We can't send him off without a feast. Just put up with that Devil, and maybe he'll give us his leftovers. Don't tell Rudolf about this—whatever happens.' That's what Stripes said."

At that instant, I heard a clink behind the door. It sounded like some metal object falling onto the floor. I looked at the door and pricked up my ears. Butchy must have heard it too. He looked at me in surprise. But no more sounds came from inside. It was quiet.

Butchy started talking again. "We went off to Devil's house. We stood on that wall and looked for the dog. There's a pond in his garden. Devil was lying in the shadow of a bush by the pond. Know what he was up to? He was waiting for a cat to come by and drink water so he could ambush it. I know because he did it to me once. When a cat comes near the water, Devil jumps onto the cat and pushes it into the pond. It's pretty deep—you could drown! In my case, I barely escaped with my life. But that's another matter.

"Anyway, when we got to his place, Devil was hiding in the bushes. Stripes called out to him, 'Hey, Devil. I've got a favor to ask you!' What do you think that pile of saggy skin and rotten teeth said?" Butchy stopped. His mouth was quivering and his eyes were glaring with anger. Then he spit out the words Devil had uttered. "'Hey, you, beggar cat! I see the scrawny one from the hardware store too. What's this favor you want to ask me? I'm in a good mood tonight. So tell me, and I might do it.'" Butchy fell silent. I didn't say a word.

A car was driving toward us with blinding headlights. As it passed by, I read the characters on the license plate—I didn't know why. "Adachi 58," it said. There were different ways to read the characters for Adachi (足立), another ward in Tokyo, and I thought about how Ippai Attena had taught me carefully so that I would get it right. I had to shake off the image though, because I started thinking about never having another lesson with my best friend.

Butchy started talking again a little more slowly. "I

was close to Stripes, so I knew he was mad. But he must have known what Devil was plotting, so he simply said, 'You're right, I'm a beggar. I'm craving beef. Spare me a little of yours, won't you?'

"Devil replied, 'My owner eats quality beef. Nothing like the beef your owner used to eat before his flight by night when he abandoned you. All right, I'll let you have some. But you know, there's no free lunch. Why don't you entertain me first, beggar cat?'

"Stripes must have been angry. I felt his rage, standing beside him. But he said, 'OK, I'll show you all my tricks. Shall I walk on my forepaws?'"

Now Butchy was choking on his words. I looked into his eyes, willing him to finish the story.

"Stripes wanted to get beef for you so badly, and Devil could sense that. 'Walking on forepaws?' he said. 'Nah, I've seen that before. Why don't you come over here and dance with your scrawny sidekick—that rackabones standing over there? Then, I'll give you all my leftovers.'

"Stripes glanced at me and whispered, 'Butchy, will you dance with me? I'll owe you big time.' How could I refuse him when he was suffering such humiliation? So I said, 'Yeah, fine with me. But are you sure you want to do this?' Stripes just nodded, but his eyes were fiery.

"Then Stripes jumped down to the ground. I followed him. I was scared, but he was walking proudly. He stood in front of Devil and asked, 'What kinda dance?'

"'Well, how about a rolling dance?' said Devil. 'Roll on your back and show me your belly.' Stripes must have sensed danger.

"'If that's what you want,' he said, 'I'd do it better alone. Butchy here will get in my way.' He gestured to me to go back. I didn't know what to do—I felt so nervous and jittery.

"'Fair enough. You, Rackabones, move away!' Devil ordered. Stripes also nodded toward me, so I jumped up on the wall and stayed there. I didn't want to see Stripes rolling and dancing for Devil, but I felt it my duty to see things through.

"Stripes lay on his back in front of Devil. Now his belly was fully exposed. He rolled over once or twice, then all of a sudden Devil jumped onto him, trying to bite into his belly. Stripes tried to avoid the attack. He quickly rolled back halfway so that Devil's teeth missed—a wound in the stomach would be fatal. But Stripes was a second late for a complete escape and Devil bit him hard on the shoulder. You saw the wound. He tried to fight back, but that horrible dog sank his fangs into Stripes' shoulder again and spun him around. Devil hurled him into the air, and he flew almost five meters over the wall and fell onto the ground in the vacant lot. I hurried to Stripes' side and found him more dead than alive. That's when I ran to fetch you."

It was so painful to listen to Butchy's story. When he was finished, I was silent, but I couldn't keep the tears from flowing.

Butchy too lapsed into silence. How long did it go on for? I don't know, but it lasted until the clinic door burst open and Mr. Bear came out. He was holding Ippai Attena, who was bandaged from head to paw.

"Have you two been waiting here all along? Boss is going to be all right. He's not in any danger, but the vet said he needs to rest for about two weeks."

That night, Mr. Bear took Ippai Attena to his apartment. Butchy and I followed. When we got to the front of the tobacco shop, our bearlike friend turned to us and asked, "Hey, want to come in too? Gee, I never knew cats could be such good friends to each other. Maybe even better than humans!"

Chapter 25

The Morning of My Departure

Mr. Bear was snoring loudly. Butchy and I stayed up all night, keeping watch over Ippai Attena. Neither of us spoke. Ippai Attena slept soundly. While it was a relief to see him resting, I was uneasy thinking he might never wake up, and I tried to ignore my fear.

At dawn, Ippai Attena's eyes opened just slightly, but they shut again before I could even say a word to him.

After some time, Mr. Bear got out of bed and found us sitting by our slumbering friend.

"Hey, cats, you've been sitting like that all night? Not a wink of sleep? Humans couldn't pull that off," he muttered to himself. Mr. Bear busied himself washing his face and brushing his teeth. Then he said, "Now I've got to go to school. You can stay here, but pee outside. I'll keep the door open a crack so you can go in and out. There's nothing here for a thief." After he left, I found a folded newspaper stuck under the door so that it wouldn't shut.

At lunchtime, Mr. Bear came back with a can of cat food. He opened it, put the food onto a plate, then went out again.

A while later, Ippai Attena's eyes opened again. When

we put our faces close to his, Ippai Attena looked at us like he couldn't see us very clearly. Then, gradually, his gaze seemed to focus. Finally he spoke.

"Where am I? Why am I here?"

"Wow, you've finally come round. It's me, Rudy. Butchy's here too."

Ippai Attena nodded, "I can see that. What kind of trouble have I caused you two? Maybe tell me later, I need a little more sleep," he said and quickly nodded off again. His breathing became even. As soon as I was sure he'd be OK, I suddenly got sleepy and drifted off.

A little later I woke up, and before I could open my eyes, I heard someone talking. The sound seemed to come from far away. I wondered who it was.

"You didn't tell Rudy anything, did you?" Someone was talking about me. "He's going home tomorrow. Don't make him worry unnecessarily."

In the evening, Mr. Bear came back with the vet in his white jacket. The vet changed Ippai Attena's bandage, expressed satisfaction with his progress, and left. Mr. Bear went off somewhere, and Butchy went to check in at home. Ippai Attena was still unable to move, but he could speak clearly.

"Rudy, sorry for the trouble. It looks like I won't be going to Gifu with you. Can you go by yourself?"

I nodded.

"Did Butchy tell you anything?"

"He said you were hit by a car," I lied. I didn't know why, maybe it was what I heard while I was half asleep.

"That's right. I don't know what I was thinking. I tried to cross the street. Didn't notice the truck. Ha, ha, ha..."

I looked down because tears were welling up in my eyes. Soon, Butchy returned, and the three of us chatted about things that didn't matter much. Evening came, but Mr. Bear didn't return.

"Where is he?" I said.

"Don't worry about that. Rudy, you need to get ready for tomorrow morning. I'm OK. Mr. Bear—and Butchy—will look after me. Don't worry about me. You've got to be going pretty soon."

It got later and later, but there was still no sign of Mr. Bear.

"Hey, Rudy, get moving. The bus leaves at six thirty. You've got to go early to see what the humans are doing. You'll have to watch for a chance to sneak on the bus," said Ippai Attena, looking concerned.

"It's too early," I replied. A rooster crowed somewhere. Where was Mr. Bear? What was he up to?

"Rudolf. Hey, Rudy. You've got to go now."

"I still have time. Don't worry about me, Ippai Attena. You sleep. I'll go when it's time."

"It's time you left. Take off now, or you'll miss the bus."

"I'm OK."

"You're not OK. Hey, Butchy. Take this brat to the bus stop."

Butchy chimed in: "Yeah, right. You should be leaving now. I'll see you off."

When I still didn't move, Ippai Attena almost shouted, "All right, Rudy. If you don't want to worry me, leave!"

I finally stood up.

"Well, Ippai Attena, you've done so much for me. Thank you."

I was unable to look him in the face. I wanted to say more, but no words came to me. Ippai Attena seemed to be looking in another direction too.

"Butchy, see me off, will you?" I asked.

Butchy went out first. I followed him out of Mr. Bear's apartment.

I might never see Ippai Attena again, I thought.

I climbed down the stairs, and started walking.

Chapter 26

Two Avengers and *Chushingura*

There was still time before daybreak. I thought I'd never be able to see Ippai Attena—or Rie or the ropeway girl. I was sad, but to tell the truth, I was much more angry than sad.

"Hey, that's the wrong way," said Butchy behind me. "You want to go to the south end of the shopping street, and that's not the way."

I ignored him and kept walking.

"Look, Rudy . . . I see that you . . . look, I know what you're thinking."

I turned around and said, "Butchy, a little after six thirty, go back to Ippai Attena and tell him that I got on the bus safely." He didn't reply but followed me silently. In another five minutes, we'd be in that empty lot next to Devil's house.

"Rudolf, let me do it with you," said Butchy. It was my turn to be silent.

"Stripes was so badly injured, and I got off without a scratch. I'm so ashamed of myself for leaving him alone to fight Devil."

We walked together quietly. Devil's garden wall was

coming into sight. When we got to it, I looked at Butchy and asked, "Ready to go in?" Butchy swallowed hard and nodded. We leaped onto the wall.

"Look," whispered Butchy. At the other end of the garden, next to the house, I saw Devil sleeping in a spot below a window, where he was sheltered by the eaves.

"Butchy, I've got an idea. Do as I say. I'll get him to chase me all over the garden. While I'm doing that, go hide in the bush by the pond. When I give you the sign, do a big jump and yowl as loudly as you can. That's all you've got to do.

"If anything happens to me, run away, Butchy. If you get hurt and nobody goes back to him, Ippai Attena will never get better. Even worse, if he figures out what's happened, he might come back to fight Devil again. If that beast kills all three of us, well that would be embarrassing. Promise me now. If Devil gets me, you'll just run away. Then tell Ippai Attena I went home to Gifu. If you can't make that promise, I won't let you help me. I'll do it by myself. What do you say?"

"OK," Butchy replied.

"All right, then. Butchy, go to the other end of the wall."

I watched Butchy trotting on the wall into the shadow of a tree. Then I cried out, "Hey, Devil. My buddies came to ask for some meat the other day. But today, I've come to take *your* meat."

Devil woke up, dragged himself to his feet, and looked in my direction. There was still time before dawn. Usually, dim light worked to my advantage, but tonight I needed to be visible. Devil was still unable to find me. I walked on the wall to the spot lit by the streetlamp.

"Hey, Devil. You cowardly canine. All you can do is play dirty tricks—even on cats," I called out.

At last the dog saw me and dashed toward me, barking. *Grrr-rr-owl, WOOF!*

I waited as Devil closed in. Just when he reached the foot of the wall, I leaped high to land as far away from him as possible. Devil turned and made a move to pounce on me. I waited a second. Then he jumped from a spot about two meters away, trying to strike me, with his jaw wide open. I darted toward him instead of backing down. Now I was dashing under Devil as he flew through the air. Devil landed badly. He may have been surprised by my feint, or he may have tried to twist his body in midair. I wanted him to sprain his leg. This was the only skill I had. Otherwise, I had no more tricks up my sleeve. Could I climb the nearest tree to escape? No, he'd catch up with me before I got there. There was nowhere to run. I turned to face Devil.

Having tumbled head over heels, the big dog was struggling to get up. He finally found his feet, but at that moment his forelegs buckled.

I did it! The horrid beast had sprained a foreleg. Now

I might be able to run as fast as him, or even faster. His speed depended upon how badly he had hurt himself. I sprinted off with my back to him.

Arf! Arf! Aarf! he barked. I kept running, and his barks sounded a little farther away each time. Every few seconds, I slowed down on purpose to delude him into thinking he could get me. I ran around the garden in all directions. I was actually trying to tire him out. Devil was already losing speed, but I wasn't in a rush. I had to make him work a little more.

I hoped Butchy was waiting in the bushes. It was almost time. I glanced back at Devil and deliberately slowed down to shorten the distance between us. Then I bolted toward the pond. The pond was so large that I'd fall in if I tried to jump straight over it. But if I veered off right before reaching the edge, Devil wouldn't be fooled. I had to jump as straight as possible across the round pond. And I needed to make a long arch so that I wouldn't fall right into the water.

One more meter to the pond. The water was glimmering with light from a nearby lamp. I saw a fallen leaf from a gingko tree floating on the surface.

Not yet. Don't jump yet, I told myself. Run toward the water. One more step, and my forepaw would touch the pond's stone border.

There! I put all my strength into my hind legs and aimed at a direction slightly forward and to the left.

Jump!

My entire body was stretched straight as an arrow. A cool, damp breeze touched my nose. I felt moisture in the air above the water. A moment before my body reached the peak of the arc, I yelled, "Now!"

Devil jumped after me at the edge of the pond. At that very instant, there was a shrill cry.

Mee-YOW! Butchy stuck out his face from the bush on the right hand side of the pond.

His cry distracted Devil, who turned toward Butchy for a split second—a serious mistake that cost him dearly. Do you know what the first rule of a jump is? Always face straight in the direction you're going.

Devil lost his balance in mid-air. He fell into the pond with a big splash and disappeared under the water.

"Butchy, when he comes up, don't let him get out. Scratch his legs, ears, everywhere. Bite him! Scratch him!"

"Got it!" Butchy yelled from the other shore. Eventually Devil's face popped up in the middle of the pond. He was swimming towards me. When he put his forepaw on the stone border, I bit into it with all my might. With a groan, Devil sank back into the water. Then his drenched face surfaced again. This time, he started wading toward the other side of the pond.

AARFF! I heard a cry from that direction. Butchy must have bitten him. We kept it up, attacking Devil every time he tried to pull himself up from the water. At last, we had him screaming for mercy, bobbing up and down in the water, sputtering.

"H-help me!"

"Help *you*? Ha! Since when are *you* entitled to ask for our help? Use your little brain," Butchy was yelling at him on the other side of the pond.

"Is th-this revenge . . . for Tiger?"

It was my turn.

"That's right. Don't think you can beg for your life. Think what you've done to our pal," I shouted.

"Please, please, help. I'm drowning . . ."

"Do it. Sink and be done with it!" Before Butchy could finish, Devil's head went under again. As he sank, I saw the metal studs on his collar glistening under the light.

The sight of his collar suddenly reminded me of the story Butchy had told me about the fight between Ippai Attena and a stray dog. Had that stray worn a collar? Why do dogs wear collars? I sometimes saw dogs taking a walk with humans. Every one of them was restrained with a leash connected to a collar.

Suddenly I understood. Stray dogs did not wear collars, nor did I. Butchy was a house cat, but wore no collar. Now I knew why Devil loathed the very sight of us strays. It was because we were free.

"Devil, promise you'll keep your hands off cats. If you

promise, we'll let you go this time," I blurted out. I didn't mean to say it, but the words just slipped out. Butchy stared at me in surprise. I was surprised too, but I felt we had had enough revenge. Ippai Attena was alive: that was all that mattered.

"There's one more thing," I added. "From now on, share your leftovers with cats. D'you promise?"

"OK, I promise." It was Devil's voice from the middle of the pond. "I'll give you leftovers. Please, don't bite me. Let me out!" Devil began to paddle towards me.

"I wish you had drowned. But my buddy let you live, so I'll spare you. You better be grateful," shouted Butchy toward Devil's back.

Devil put his paws on a stone at the rim of the pond. As he tried to pull himself up, I bit into his ear hard. "Remember how much it hurts," I spit out.

Butchy was by my side, and our victory was absolute. Devil was soaking wet, gripping the stone and panting heavily. His hind quarters were still in the water, his ears were plastered to his face, and he was bleeding from my bite. *Now is the perfect timing for that line!* I was about to say it, but Butchy was ahead of me. "You're hardly worth the breath, but I'm warning you to never touch another hair on the head of a cat. Next time I'll bite off both your ears, and you'll look like a rat in a ski cap!"

The sun was coming up. Butchy and I jumped over the wall.

"We've done it. Just like *Chushingura*!" said Butchy. I had heard from Ippai Attena about *Chushingura*, the story of forty-seven samurai, who took revenge for their former lord's dishonorable death.

"Now let's go back and tell Ippai Attena all about what we've done," I said and began trotting back toward the tobacco shop.

"Wait, Rudy, the bus is leaving pretty soon. If you go back to see Stripes, you'll miss it," said Butchy behind me. I turned around.

"What're you talking about?" I replied. "When I saw Ippai Attena injured, I decided not to get on that bus. I can go home any time I want. I can even walk home if I have to. Who knows? There may even be another bus trip someday. There's no rush. And, you know, I want to learn more from our friend."

The night sky was suddenly light, and the morning sun was beginning to warm our backs as we hurried off to see Ippai Attena.

Author's Afterword

I was coming home one day, and I heard the phone ringing from inside the house. I opened the door, almost tripping over a messy pile of paper someone had left there, and hurried inside.

"Have you read it?" asked the caller, a friend of mine.

"Read what?" I asked.

"I put it in front of your door."

I realized my friend was referring to that untidy bundle of paper.

"If you haven't read it yet, do it by tomorrow," commanded the caller, and hung up.

I untied the bundle and found what appeared to be a manuscript written on all kinds of paper—newspaper flyers, pages torn out of notebooks, and even wrapping paper from department stores. Each piece was covered in writing of all sizes—small and large. As you might already have guessed, that manuscript turned into this book.

There was another call from the same friend the next morning. I learned that my pal had stumbled across the manuscript somewhere, and that it was actually the autobiography of a cat. He wanted me to find a publisher and make it into a book. I told him to do it on his own.

"Don't be ridiculous. No one would believe me if I told them I had a story written by a cat. They'd think I was nuts," he replied.

"I don't want anyone calling me crazy either," I protested.

"Then just say you wrote it yourself. Look, I'm too busy to deal with it, so I'm counting on you!" My friend hung up, and that was the end of the matter.

In the days that followed, though, I pondered the mysterious manuscript. Finally I made a fair copy of it, gave it the title *Rudolf and Ippai Attena*, and entered it into the contest for the Kodansha Children's Literature New Writer Award. It was a big surprise when the story won and Kodansha announced they would publish it.

Of course, I kept the real author a secret. But I couldn't keep the secret forever, and one day I decided to confess everything to my editor at Kodansha.

"To tell you the truth, a cat wrote this . . ." I began.

"Don't worry," the editor said with a patient smile. "We'll make it into a nice book."

I was never sure if the editor believed me, but of course adults would never believe a cat could write a book.

Hiroshi Saito
Tokyo

Notes

P.5 9 an alien from outer space 宇宙人 11 be shocked speechless 口もきけないくらいびっくりする 13 happened to ... たまたま〜した 16 floating in mid-air 宙に浮いている 18 don't get me wrong 誤解しないで 18 eye-opener 目を見張るもの 19 every once in a while たまに

P.6 3 reflect light and shine blue 光を反射して青く光る 4 Got it yet? もうわかった? 7 cynical 懐疑的 9 the earth orbited the sun 地球が太陽の周りを回っている 9 not the other way around その逆ではない 11 got hopping mad カンカンに怒った

P.7 2 Rats! しまった! 4 scarf ... down 〜をがつがつ食べる 5 smelt ししゃも 9 wasn't going for ... 〜を狙っていない 11 knock me right out 一発で気絶する 15 limp away 足を引きずって逃げる 16 lethal 致命的 18 hightail it 急いで逃げる 18 dodge to the left or the right 右に左に身をかわしてすばやく避ける

P.8 3 good bet かなり確かなこと 4 slip in 滑り込む 4 be home free 安全圏に入る 7 zipped through 勢いよく走

り抜けた　**9** pointy heel 尖ったヒール　**10** fishmonger 魚屋　**10** launched 投げつけた　**13** hit a nerve 神経に障った　**15** alley 路地　**18** small talk おしゃべり　**20** took a wide right 右に大きく曲がった　**25** dead end 行き止まり

P.9 　**2** whipped around くるりと振り向いた　**3** tripped つまずいた　**5** pursuer 追っ手　**18** unintelligibly 不明朗に　**19** revved up 回転数が上がった　**20** The truck pulled away from the curb. 縁石に止まっていたトラックが発車した　**22** whapped 強く打った　**24** drone 低く続くブーンという音

P.10 　**5** mind was foggy 頭がぼんやりしていた　**8** figured 思った　**8** willing myself up 思い切って立ち上がろうとして　**9** wobbled よろめいた　**15** dim 薄暗い　**17** managed to . . . 何とか〜した　**18** I made my unsteady way towards . . . ふらふらしながら〜に向かって進んだ

P.11 　**5** scenery racing by 飛ぶように過ぎていく景色　**5** completely unfamiliar まったく見覚えがない　**6** something else bothered me 他にも気になることがあった　**7** I couldn't quite put my finger on it それが何かは、はっきりしなかった　**8** figured it out 考えついた

P.12 　**2** my human's house ぼくの飼い主の家　**22** carried me on board ぼくを抱いて乗った　**24** swayed 揺れた　**25** mountain peak 山頂

P.13　6 too huge to even compare 比べ物にならないくらい大きい　11 at an angle 斜めに

P.14　10 the coast was clear 危険はない　15 took a left 左に曲がった　17 stroll 散歩　19 land 着地する　19 growled 低い声で言った　21 fight-or-flight 闘うか逃げるか

P.15　2 cut . . . off 〜の進行を妨げる　4 promising 期待のもてる　8 not from around here この辺りの者ではない　14 split . . . 〜を分け合う　17 gigantic 巨大な　18 shaking . . . down 〜から脅し取ろうとしている　19 new tack 新しいやり方　24 humiliating 屈辱的　25 It's every beast for himself. 誰にも頼れない状況だ　27 avoid 避ける

P.16　3 lug のろま　4 lack of attention 注意不足　6 bandits 山賊　7 bullies いじめっ子　8 pick on . . . 〜をいじめる　9 bound to . . . 〜するに違いない　17 claws 爪　19 judging from . . . 〜から判断すると　20 running start 助走　22 change direction once in mid-air 空中で一回向きを変える　24 feint left 左に行くようなふりをする　26 enormous gut 大きな腹　27 sprain a leg or two 足を一本か二本くじく

P.17　7 Like I'd ever fall for that old trick. そんな手には引っ掛からない　12 wasn't budging てこでも動かない　16 brat がき

P.18　4 within reach of . . . 〜に手の届くところ　4 cringed

体を縮こまらせた　8 talk tough 強がりを言う　8 give you credit for... 〜はほめてやる　10 shrimp ちび　13 What was the deal with... 〜はいったいどういうつもりなんだ　16 back down 引き下がる　17 lunk ばか　19 hold your horses ちょっと待て　19 odd job へんなやつ

P.19 2 *ippai attena* いっぱいあってな　12 squirt ちび　13 reputation 名声　14 itsy bitsy ちっぽけな　17 mouthing off 言いふらす　17 cronies 仲間　20 trotted 小走りに歩いた

P.20 3 faces start to balloon 顔がふくらんでくる　5 impressive 堂々とした　10 tiger cats トラねこ　17 yowled 大声で鳴いた　19 half pint とても小さい者　20 Whaddaya (What do you) mean? どういう意味だよ？

P.21 3 dimwit まぬけ　5 big shot 大物　5 treat me to a meal ごちそうしてくれる　8 knucklehead まぬけ　10 squid イカ　12 anxious がっついている　13 bait breath（釣り針に仕掛ける）えさのにおいがする息　21 broken-down 壊れかかった　22 one-story house 一階建ての家　24 duct tape ビニールテープ　25 cave in 崩れ落ちる　26 half-hearted 中途半端な

P.22 2 tattered ぼろぼろになった　5 paw（かぎ爪のある動物の）足　9 work up an appetite おなかをすかせる　10 haunted house おばけ屋敷　12 screech 甲高い声をあげる　14 ruckus 大騒ぎ　19 dingy 薄暗い　20 hunched-over 猫背の　20 hag 醜い老婆　22 racket

騒音　**24 bonafide** 本物の　**24 witch** 魔女　**26 do . . . bidding** 〜の命令に従う

P.23　**2 simmer** グツグツ煮る　**5 my legs gave out from under me** 腰を抜かしてしまった　**11 put a spell on . . .** 〜に魔法をかける　**12 recite some kind of magic words** 呪文をかける　**21 broth** だし　**23 lovesick** 恋わずらいの　**24 tree trunks** 木の幹

P.24　**15 gruff attitude** 不愛想な態度　**17 creaked** ギーと鳴った　**20 saw** のこぎり　**20 ax** おの

P.25　**7 stray** のら（ねこ）　**8 dried sardine** 煮干し　**11 munching away** むしゃむしゃ食べている　**14 polished . . . off** 〜を素早く平らげた　**19 chatting** おしゃべりしている

P.26　**6 getting on . . . nerves** 〜をイライラさせている　**10 numbskull** ばか者　**12 insisted** 主張した、むきになって言った

P.27　**1 that's too rich** これはけっさくだ　**17 filthy** 不潔な　**18 good for a bite or two** 何か食べさせてくれる　**25 the likes of you** おまえのようなやつ

P.28　**3 determined to . . .** 〜と決心している　**21 pin . . . down** 突き止める

P.29　**10 concluded** 結論を出した

P.30　**2 well up** 湧き上がる　**3 blubbering** 泣きじゃくること　**3 what the heck** 仕方ない　**4 look after . . .** 〜の面倒

P.31 を見る 6 puny 取るに足りない 9 soggy びしょ濡れの

P.31 4 my sinking heart was suddenly lifted ゆううつな気分がいっぺんで吹き飛んだ 7 revived 復活した 16 snuck . . . into ～をこっそり入れた

P.32 10 it was news to me that . . . ～なんて初めて知った 16 plump ぽっちゃりした 20 beats me まったくわからない 25 runt ちび（の動物） 25 tagging along 付いてきている 27 How rude なんて失礼な

P.33 4 calico cats 三毛ねこ 21 glared at . . . ～をにらみつけた 22 superstition 迷信 23 education 教養

P.34 2 declared 宣言した 5 be lumped with . . . ～といっしょにされる 7 hold your temper 怒るな 7 Tokyoites 東京人（江戸っ子） 13 grumpy 不機嫌な

P.35 3 leftovers 残飯 5 bonito flakes かつお節 13 exhausted 疲れ切った 19 have their eye out for . . . ～に目を光らせている

P.36 1 mischievous いたずらっぽい 1 I rolled my eyes. ぼくはあきれた顔をした 7 had no business . . . ～に用はない 13 scrubber たわし 26 meowed ニャオーと鳴いた 27 . . . was a goner ～は救いようがない

P.37 4 startle びっくりさせる 4 chided 叱った 5 move, wouldja (would you) どいてくれないか 10 ever so slightly ほんのわずかに 11 beckoned me over ぼくを手招きした 26 rotten 腐った

P.38 **2** play the role of ...の役を演じる

P.39 **2** shrine 神社　**16** Rudolf I of Habsburg ハプスブルク家のルドルフ一世

P.40 **14** now that you mention it そういえば　**22** play nice 仲良くする

P.41 **8** flopped down on his side ごろりと横になった　**14** pick and choose えりすぐる　**17** stay on the offensive ずっと攻勢に出ている　**22** flipped over on his side さっとひっくり返った

P.42 **2** shed a tear or two 涙を一粒か二粒流す

P.43 **2** wilt しおれる　**3** didn't have a clue 手がかりが何もなかった　**16** cheeky ずうずうしい

P.44 **2** under her eaves 彼女の家の軒先　**6** vet (veterinarian) 獣医　**8** wet as a dishrag ずぶ濡れになって　**13** sopping wet びしょ濡れ　**22** saucer 小さな皿

P.45 **3** Hold on there! ちょっと待って！　**3** choke 喉につかえる　**7** until the rain lets up 雨があがるまで

P.46 **1** stroking my back ぼくの背中をなでて　**10** blurry ぼやけた

P.47 **15** rainy season 梅雨

P.48 **2** destination 目的地　**4** sparrow すずめ　**7** ran parallel to ... 〜と平行する　**7** sprouted 葉が生え始めた　**19** tabby cat ブチねこ　**27** Whaddaya (What do you)

know. それは驚いた

P.49　1 neither here nor there 取るに足りない、どうでもいいこと　8 remark 発言　11 hardware shop 金物屋　16 impatiently いらいらして

P.50　5 bugged いらいらさせた　12 That was a relief. それを知って安心した　24 any old cat どんなねこでも　25 what kind of trap they had laid どんなわなが仕掛けられているか

P.51　2 nailed ぶちのめした　3 accidentally うっかりと　3 got a few punches in 何発かパンチを食らわせた

P.52　10 narrative 物語　17 nasty piece of work いやなやつ　20 mutt ばか、野良犬

P.53　1 hunkered down しゃがんだ　3 one-hundredth of a second 100分の1秒　4 at a diagonal 斜めに　10 hold on a sec (second) ちょっと待って　10 interrupted ...と言って話をさえぎった　13 eagerly 熱心に　16 gone blind 失明した　17 vision 視力

P.54　1 yelping キャンキャンほえて　3 you're hardly worth the breath おまえに言うのも無駄だ　18 line せりふ　26 human owner 飼い主の人間

P.55　6 I was barely listening. ほとんど聞いていなかった　17 cooed クークー鳴いた　19 Showed you! 見たか！

P.56　7 marched off 堂々と歩いていった　11 alternated with ...～と交互にあった　16 didn't seem particularly interested 特に興味はないようだった

P.57 **20** the difference between victory and defeat 勝敗の分かれ目　**23** light on... ～に舞い降りる　**24** pounce on... ～に襲いかかる

P.58 **6** horizontal bars 鉄棒　**6** his back was to me 彼はこちらに背中を向けていた　**14** gravelly ざらついた

P.59 **3** voice cracked 声がかすれた　**14** smarted ずきずき痛んだ　**16** got a smart mouth 口が達者である　**18** mimic 真似する　**21** high and mighty 偉そうな　**22** sophisticated 洗練された

P.60 **3** classy しゃれた　**4** crass 粗野な　**5** in my own defense 自分の弁護のために　**8** particular occasion 特定の出来事　**8** get a point across 言いたいことを人に分からせる　**10** pass the time ひまをつぶす

P.61 **2** think better of... ～を考え直す

P.62 **7** gingko tree イチョウの木　**14** hung in flaps ひだになって垂れていた　**16** greedy 欲張りな

P.63 **3** vacant lot 空き地　**22** You don't say. まさか

P.64 **15** cove 入江　**17** continent 大陸

P.65 **6** get by on your own 自力で何とかやっていく　**10** made my exit 退場した　**20** character 文字

P.67 **8** dumbfounded ものが言えないほどびっくりした

P.69 **10** scoffed あざ笑った　**12** irritated いらいらした　**17**

volume 書籍　**27** call it a day おしまいにする

P.70　**3** biography 伝記　**8** smirked にやにや笑った

P.71　**5** crept through こっそり通り抜けた　**14** burglars 泥棒

P.72　**11** educated 教養のある

P.73　**4** partway through 途中で

P.74　**15** reviewed 復習した　**16** syllabary 字音表

P.75　**8** plopped down ドスンと座った　**12** no good can come out of... ～してもろくなことはない　**14** blunt 遠慮のない　**20** kept at it やっていることを続けた

P.76　**7** to boot おまけに　**26** Now you're gonna get it! こうしてやる！

P.78　**1** muggy 蒸し暑い　**8** it's not what I'm getting at そういうことを言おうとしているんじゃない　**13** patient 辛抱強い　**16** sneak into 忍び込む

P.79　**7** muttered ぶつぶつ言った　**9** scavenge あさる　**13** slept in 朝寝した　**18** nonchalantly 無頓着に　**26** lost-and-found 遺失物

P.80　**3** talking in riddles 謎めいた話し方をしている　**9** social skills 社交術　**13** faculty room 職員室　**16** feigned innocence 無邪気なふり　**17** feline innocence ねこの無邪気さ　**27** beard あごひげ

P.81　**3** tied up with... ～で忙しくて手が離せない　**21** vary 変化をつける

P.82　**12** teach him tricks 芸を教える　**17** doorpost 戸口の側柱　**21** halted 立ち止まった　**26** repetitions 繰り返し

P.83　**4** oddball 変わり者　**12** bird brain ばか者　**15** pronto すぐに　**16** what he was up to 彼が何をたくらんでいるか　**20** ringleader （サーカスの）舞台監督　**20** circus troupe サーカス団

P.84　**14** bundle of keys 鍵の束　**15** jabbed 突き刺した

P.85　**10** spectacular 壮観な　**18** Awesome! すごい！　**18** crowed キャッキャッと声をあげた　**19** thrilled わくわくしている　**26** let the cat out of the bag うっかり秘密を漏らす　**27** under . . . nose 〜の目の前で

P.86　**21** rag on . . . 〜をからかう　**22** stuck up うぬぼれている

P.87　**2** mischief いたずら　**15** Humans didn't seem to be capable of much progress either. 人間もあまり進歩しているようには見えなかった

P.88　**11** expect . . . 〜（が来ること）を待つ　**19** went bad 腐った

P.89　**3** tailed . . . 〜のあとをつけた　**5** at a distance 少し離れて　**22** tap 水道

P.90　**1** ignorant 無知　**13** bear's den くまの洞穴　**13** Resi-DEN-ce (residence) 住まい

P.91　**5** uneducated 教養がない　**6** just a slip 口が滑っただけ　**7** hubby (husband) 夫　**17** darted off 駆け去った

P.93 2 you must've got something between your ears おまえは頭が空っぽではないはずだ　15 vast expanse of water 広大な海原　16 opposite shore 向こう岸　18 panned （テレビカメラが）ゆっくりと左右に動いた　18 dotted with . . . 〜が点在している　19 wiggling ぴくぴく動いている　21 cutlassfish タチウオ　23 drowsy 眠い　27 glimpse ちらりと見る

P.94 1 cormorant fishing 鵜飼い　4 baffled 当惑した　7 riveted to . . . 〜にくぎ付けになる　23 bubbling over with . . . 〜にあふれている　24 babbled ベラベラしゃべった

P.95 20 landed neatly on all fours 四本脚できれいに着地した

P.97 6 vehicles 乗り物　20 outskirts 郊外　21 tricky 難しい

P.98 4 stops 停車駅　7 snags 障害　9 conductor 車掌　13 freight train 貨物列車　16 roofless 屋根のない　17 container cars コンテナー車　27 guarantee 保証

P.99 1 load and unload 積み下ろしをする　12 despair is the solace of fools 絶望は、おろか者の答え　14 don't rush to conclusions 結論を急ぐな　18 drifted off 眠りに落ちた　23 hopes and disappointments 期待と失望

P.100 22 pry 詮索する　25 puzzled 戸惑った

P.101 4 shook me up 動揺させられた

P.102 7 connected by land 地続き　9 offended 気分を害した

9 think otherwise 別の考えを持つ   15 if worst came to worst 最悪の場合には   15 resolved 決心した   21 all my efforts would be wasted すべての努力が無駄になる

P.103 1 typhoons 台風   3 raged 猛威を振るった   3 drove 強打した   7 flooded 水浸しになった   9 blustery 荒れ狂っている   14 fled to safety 避難した   15 hold 持ちこたえる   19 when push comes to shove いざとなったら

P.104 2 confessed 打ち明けた   3 gee おや   4 be in such a fix こんな困ったことになる   26 peel ... off ～をはがす

P.105 4 wriggle 身をよじる   8 squirming もがく、身をよじる   10 suffocating 息が詰まって   16 cracked up 爆笑した   17 hilarious 笑える   21 pushpins 画びょう   27 misfortunes 不幸

P.106 2 Jeez ちぇっ   2 crabby 怒りっぽい   4 human race 人類   5 no inkling 夢にも思わなかった   8 pulling my leg ぼくをからかっている   16 feast ごちそう   21 carp コイ

P.107 1 became fainter 弱くなった   13 followed his gaze 彼の視線を追った   13 whitish 白っぽい

P.108 14 nooks and crannies 隅々

P.109 2 miserable 情けない   12 gorge ガツガツ食べる   13 get on great とても仲良くしている   16 squatted しゃが

んだ　**16** purred 喉をゴロゴロ鳴らした

P.110　**5** bawled 怒鳴った　**6** creeping up on... ～に忍び寄って　**15** gather momentum 弾みをつける　**16** barred his way 彼の行く手を遮った　**19** cowered 縮こまった　**22** abandoned cats 捨てねこ

P.111　**1** a split second 一瞬　**2** hurled 放り投げられた　**3** ditch どぶ　**19** butted in 口を出した　**26** sauntered off ぶらぶらと去っていった

P.112　**9** dubious いぶかしげ　**12** local merchants' association 地元の商店会　**17** tilted his head 彼は首をかしげた

P.113　**16** lay off かまうのをやめる　**17** There's no telling what he'll do when he goes off like that. あいつは頭に血がのぼると何をするかわからない

P.114　**2** rough up 痛めつける　**6** back to square one 振り出しに戻った　**6** assumed... ～と想定した　**17** clung to a thread of hope わずかな希望を捨てなかった

P.115　Hard-luck Story かわいそうな身の上話　**18** sniffed 鼻であしらった　**21** murmured つぶやいた

P.116　**3** trying to sound casual 平静さを装って　**6** bluntly そっけなく　**16** itching to... ～するのにうずうずしていた

P.117　**1** bowed and scraped ぺこぺこした　**6** too naïve 考えが甘すぎた　**8** they changed their attitudes completely 彼らは完全に態度を変えた　**14** hate even the sight of... ~を見るのも嫌だ 17 hedge 生け垣 19 runs around loose 放し飼いになっている 21 cajoled... into... ~をおだてて~させた 25 bloodshot 血走った

P.118　1 beast けだもの 2 despise ひどく嫌う 3 put up with... ~に耐える 5 blurted out 思わず口走った 13 forced the stuff down 無理して食べた 14 puked it up 吐いた 14 eyes smoldered with hatred 目には憎しみが燃えていた 17 hardship 苦労 26 Ahoy! おーい!

P.119　11 like a shot 弾丸のように

P.120　7 zip 疾走する 7 made way for... ~に道を譲った 8 charged 突進した 11 D'ya (Do you) think cats race? ねこも競争するのかな? 18 pharmacy 薬局 26 chartered bus 貸し切りバス 27 transfer 乗り換える

P.121　6 in high spirits 意気揚々として 9 wailing 叫んでいる 9 sniffling 鼻をすすって 14 baggage compartment 手荷物棚 18 coward 臆病者 20 getting carried away 興奮している 24 carsick 車酔い

P.122　10 cuddled up 抱かれて 12 strolling ぶらついて 16 hanging out with a bad crowd 悪い連中とつるんでいる 17 kicking up a din 大騒ぎして

P.123　4 littering 散らかっている 18 thumped ドシンと落ちた

P.125　7 as if reading my mind ぼくの心を読んだように 10 now or never 今でなければ二度とない 13 errands 用

P.126 事

18 so saying そう言うと　24 scattered 散らばっていた　25 bristles (筆の) 毛

P.127 4 Lo and behold 驚いたことに、そしてなんと　6 exchanged glances 顔を見合わせた　21 sit for me (絵の) モデルになってくれ

P.128 Foul Play 反則　14 distract 気を散らす　15 art of self-defense 護身術

P.129 19 we were well into autumn 秋が深まっていた　20 chilly ひんやりする　21 debated whether . . . ～かどうか思案した

P.130 8 agitated 動揺している　10 played a dirty trick 卑劣な手を使った

P.131 4 triumphantly 勝ち誇って　15 bolted 駆け出した　20 not even a twitch ピクリともしない　21 slimy ぬるぬるした

P.132 18 tumbling 転がって　19 pace slackening ペースが落ちている

P.133 2 at the top of my lungs 声を限りに　9 make . . . out ～を見分ける　10 regretted 残念に思った　11 vending machine 自動販売機

P.134 8 It's been ages. 遅かったじゃないか　24 dress a wound 傷の手当をする

P.135 1 on . . . trail ～の跡を追って　4 passers-by 通行人

P.136 2 come to think of it 考えてみれば　6 spare 分け与える　9 with his eyes downcast 目を伏せて　22 pricked up my ears 聞き耳を立てた

P.137 3 ambush 待ち伏せして襲う　10 pile of saggy skin and rotten teeth 垂れた皮膚と腐った歯の山　13 uttered 口にした　14 beggar 物もらい　14 scrawny やせこけた

P.138 3 craving . . . ～が欲しくてたまらない　6 flight by night 夜逃げ　8 there's no free lunch ただでもらえる物はない　12 forepaws 前足　18 sidekick 仲間　19 rackabones 骨と皮だけのように痩せこけた動物　22 I'll owe you big time. 一生、恩にきる　23 humiliation 屈辱　25 fiery 燃えている

P.139 8 jittery 神経が立っている　12 duty 義務　12 see things through 最後まで見届ける　15 exposed 露出している　19 fatal 致命的　22 fangs 牙

P.140 4 lapsed into silence 黙り込んだ

P.141 3 slept soundly ぐっすり眠った　9 slumbering 眠っている　10 Not a wink of sleep 一睡もしなかった　11 pull . . . off ～をうまくやる

P.142 5 come round 意識を回復する　9 nodded off 眠った

P.143 20 looking concerned 心配そうな顔をして　21 rooster にわとり　21 crowed 鳴いた

P.144 4 chimed in 相づちを打った　5 see . . . off ～を見送る

P.145 **18** got off without a scratch かすり傷も負わずにすんだ

P.146 **2** swallowed hard ごくりと唾を飲んだ

P.147 **6** canine 犬 **10** closed in 迫ってきた **20** I had no more tricks up my sleeve 隠し持っている切り札はもうなかった **24** tumbled head over heels 真っ逆さまに転がった **26** forelegs buckled 前脚が曲がって倒れた

P.148 **6** delude 惑わす **12** deliberately わざと **15** veered off それた **26** hind legs 後ろ脚

P.149 **2** straight as an arrow 一本の矢のように **3** moisture 湿り気 **11** cost . . . dearly 〜は大きな代償を払った **24** drenched ずぶ濡れの **24** surfaced 水中から浮上した **25** wading 水の中を歩いて

P.150 **2** screaming for mercy 勘弁してくれと叫びながら **2** bobbing up and down あっぷあっぷして **3** sputtering 口から水を飛ばして **5** entitled to . . . 〜する権利がある **10** beg for your life 命乞いをする **15** studs 飾りびょう **15** glistening 濡れて光っている **21** restrained 拘束されている **22** leash リード **25** loathed the very sight of . . . 〜を見るのも嫌なほど憎んでいる

P.151 **12** be grateful 感謝する **17** absolute 絶対的 **19** hind quarters 下半身 **20** plastered to . . . 〜に貼り付いている

P.152 **4** lord 藩主 **4** dishonorable 不名誉な

P.154 **8** untidy 乱雑な **11** commanded 命令した **13** manuscript 原稿　**13** flyers チラシ　**19** stumbled across... 〜を偶然見つけた　**21** autobiography 自伝

P.155　**2** Don't be ridiculous. ばかを言うな　**8** I'm counting on you! 頼りにしているからな！　**10** pondered... 〜についてじっくり考えた　**11** made a fair copy 清書した　**16** author 著者

（後註執筆・星野真理／翻訳家）

KODANSHA ENGLISH LIBRARY

ルドルフとイッパイアッテナ
Rudolf and Ippai Attena

2017年4月20日	第1刷発行
2024年3月13日	第2刷発行

著 者	斉藤 洋（さいとう ひろし）
訳 者	岩渕 デボラ（いわぶち）、遠田 和子（えんだ かずこ）
発行者	清田 則子
発行所	株式会社講談社
	〒112-8001　東京都文京区音羽2-12-21
	販売　東京 03-5395-3606
	業務　東京 03-5395-3615
編 集	株式会社講談社エディトリアル
	代表　堺 公江
	〒112-0013　東京都文京区音羽1-17-18 護国寺SIAビル
	編集部　東京 03-5319-2171
本文DTP	ギルド
印刷・製本所	大日本印刷株式会社

KODANSHA

落丁本・乱丁本は購入書店名を明記のうえ、講談社業務宛にお送りください。送料小社負担にてお取り替えいたします。なお、この本についてのお問い合わせは、講談社エディトリアル宛にお願いいたします。本書のコピー、スキャン、デジタル化等の無断複製は著作権法上での例外を除き禁じられています。本書を代行業者等の第三者に依頼してスキャンやデジタル化することはたとえ個人や家庭内の利用でも著作権法違反です。

定価はカバーに表示してあります。

©2017 Hiroshi Saito, Deborah Iwabuchi, Kazuko Enda
Printed in Japan
ISBN 978-4-06-250088-3